THE LOST CANYON OF GOLD

The Discovery of the Legendary Lost Adams Diggings

W. C. Jameson

TWODOT®

Guilford, Connecticut
Helena, Montana

TWODOT®

An imprint of Globe Pequot
An imprint and registered trademark of Rowman & Littlefield

Copyright © 2017 by W. C. Jameson
All photographs provided by author

British Library Cataloguing in Publication Information Available

Library of Congress Cataloging-in-Publication Data Available
ISBN 978-1-63076-176-9 (pbk : alk. paper)
ISBN 978-1-4930-3115-3 (electronic)

OTHER BOOKS BY W. C. JAMESON

Buried Treasures of America Series

The Silver Madonna and Other Tales of America's Greatest Lost Treasures
Finding Treasure: A Field Guide
Treasure Hunter: Caches, Curses, and Deadly Confrontations
Buried Treasures of the American Southwest
Buried Treasures of Texas
Buried Treasures of the Ozarks
Buried Treasures of the Appalachians
Buried Treasures of California
Buried Treasures of the Rocky Mountain West
Buried Treasures of the Great Plains
Buried Treasures of the South
Buried Treasures of the Pacific Northwest
Buried Treasures of New England
Buried Treasures of the Atlantic Coast
Buried Treasures of the Mid-Atlantic States
Buried Treasures of the Ozarks and Appalachians
New Mexico Treasure Tales
Colorado Treasure Tales
Lost Mines and Buried Treasures of Arizona
Lost Mines and Buried Treasures of Old Wyoming
Lost Mines and Buried Treasures of Arkansas
Lost Mines and Buried Treasures of Missouri
Lost Mines and Buried Treasures of Tennessee
Lost Mines and Buried Treasures of Oklahoma
Texas Tales of Lost Mines and Buried Treasures
Legend and Lore of the Guadalupe Mountains
Lost Mines and Buried Treasures of the Guadalupe Mountains
Lost Mines and Buried Treasures of the Big Bend
Lost Treasures in American History
Lost Treasures of Arkansas's Waterways
Lost Mines and Buried Treasures of the Civil War
Outlaw Treasures (audio)
Buried Treasures of the Civil War (audio)

Beyond the Grave Series

Amelia Earhart: Beyond the Grave
John Wilkes Booth: Beyond the Grave
Butch Cassidy: Beyond the Grave
Billy the Kid: Beyond the Grave
Billy the Kid: The Lost Interviews
The Return of the Assassin, John Wilkes Booth

Books on Writing

The Seven Keys to Becoming a Successful Writer
An Elevated View: Colorado Writers on Writing
Hot Coffee and Cold Truth: Living and Writing the West
Notes from Texas: On Writing in the Lone Star State
Want to Be a Successful Writer? Do This Stuff

Poetry

Bones of the Mountain
I Missed the Train to Little Rock
Open Range: Poetry of the Re-imagined West
(edited with Laurie Wagner Buyer)

Food

Chili from the Southwest
The Ultimate Chili Cookbook
Tex-Americana Fandango Cookbook

Fiction

Keep the Bullets Flying
Eulogy
Beating the Devil

Other

Pat Garrett: The Man behind the Badge
Unsolved Mysteries of the Old West
A Sense of Place: Essays on the Ozarks
Ozark Tales of Ghosts, Spirits, Hauntings, and Monsters
Ozark Folk Wisdom

For Jim Peterson for showing the way,
and for Laurie, as always

Contents

Part IV: The Rediscovery of the Lost Adams Diggings

Prologue

From the moment I first set foot in the canyon I was overwhelmed by the sensation that, after more than four decades of searching, I had finally found it—the location of the legendary Lost Adams Diggings, which many consider to have been the richest streambed accumulation of gold nuggets anywhere in the Northern Hemisphere. The feeling gathered momentum, grew, surged, and consumed me.

The trail was rocky, winding across the stream channel and the low banks. Though it was early afternoon, the canyon was shaded to a curious darkness by the large sycamore and Emory oak trees that thrived throughout. Along the sides of the canyon, piñon pine and Arizona cypress flourished. Pine jays scolded. The only other sound was the hum of insects and the crunch of the gravel beneath hiking boots. Here and there could be found fresh piles of bear scat, and the slight breeze carried the gamey scent of the animal from somewhere ahead of me.

Intuition aside, however, I could only determine the validity of my presumed discovery, my claim that I was standing in the legendary canyon, by locating and identifying a number of geographic and cultural features that would provide pertinent evidence. These included the zigzag canyon, the rock hearth with the secret chamber, the remains of a burnt log cabin, a waterfall, an Apache campground, and, most importantly, the presence of gold in the stream.

Over several generations, dozens and perhaps hundreds have claimed to have found the fabled Lost Adams Diggings. I had listened to accounts and read stories, but they left me disappointed. While all the claims were accompanied by enthusiasm and excitement, none provided any actual proof, or even pertinent evidence, that the so-called finders of the rich placer deposit had accomplished what they had set out to do. In the end I determined that the others were mistaken, confused, or simply not telling the truth. A curious common element associated with almost every one of the alleged discoveries was that none of them included the presence of gold. Even as a young man in my twenties, I was not persuaded by any of these accounts, and I decided to pursue my own search with renewed vigor. I knew in my heart that the elusive canyon of gold still waited to be found, studied, and verified. I kept searching.

After four decades of reading, researching, and investigating, as well as deconstructing and reconstructing the tale and the evidence, all accompanied by a number of expeditions to the purported site, I was convinced I was in the correct canyon, the one found by the man Adams and his partners over a century and a half earlier, the one from which a fortune in gold nuggets had been gleaned. If even half of the tales were true, gold should still be present in the streambed, nuggets large enough and of a sufficient quantity to surrender to the patient miner.

I continued following the dim trail, crossing and recrossing the stream. If I were accurate in my calculations, everything I needed to see and know, to prove that this was the famous lost canyon, would be apparent within the next hour.

Introduction

Throughout the written and oral history of almost all of the world's cultures, there exist uncountable tales and legends of lost mines and buried treasures, along with accounts of grand quests to locate them. The promise of finding great wealth that has been lost or hidden is, and always has been, compelling enough to attract millions to the search over the centuries.

Riches in the form of gold, silver, and precious stones are alluring, to be sure, but for many it is the quest, the journey, that is important. True, there may be a fortune waiting at the end, but it is the adventure that keeps the daring, the enterprising, and the courageous returning over and over. Few men with a full quota of spirit and a zest for life can resist such a call.

The pursuit of lost treasure can represent many things: a slice of life out of the ordinary, an escape from the mundanity of the daily job, relief from an unfulfilled life, the pursuit of riches. It is the quest that fills the void—spiritual, emotional, intellectual, and physical. The strength of this appeal is no less today than it was during the time of Jason and the Argonauts when they hunted for the Golden Fleece, no less than that which challenged the Vikings to cross the Atlantic Ocean in wooden boats and set out to explore the North American continent, no less than American men of the mid-nineteenth century who journeyed westward on foot and horseback, by train and wagon, in search of gold in the rocky outcrops of the California sierras.

The pursuit of treasure has enticed men to journey to distant places, to unknown lands filled with exotic cultures. Many of these tales have been handed down over the millennia. Some of the most memorable historical and contemporary written works have addressed this topic. Books such as Homer's *The Odyssey* and Robert Louis Stevenson's *Treasure Island* have thrilled millions of readers for generations. More recently, the film adventures of Indiana Jones and Clive Cussler's thriller novels detailing the treasure hunts and escapades of the fictional Dirk Pitt continue to invite and enchant. The iconic Texas folklorist and writer J. Frank Dobie collected and chronicled dozens of tales of lost mines and buried treasures located in the United States and Mexico. Dobie, in fact, is probably more responsible than anyone for introducing some of the more famous lost-treasure legends to readers.

The search for treasure need not always take place in foreign and exotic lands, on remote islands, or in dangerous environments. Many of the world's most fascinating tales are set in the United States. Here, thousands of long-forgotten mines and hidden caches of gold and silver coins and ingots, as well as precious stones, exist from coast to coast, border to border. Most readers are familiar with the oft-told tale of the lost Dutchman's gold of the Superstition Mountains and the elusive treasure of Oak Island not far from the coast of Maine, but for every one of these high-profile treasures, there are hundreds more that are unknown to the public. Any one of them has the potential to yield its location to the patient and diligent researcher.

One story, a tale that involves what may be the richest placer gold deposit in the United States, lies in a narrow canyon within a dozen miles of a small town of approximately twenty-two hundred citizens and only an hour's hike from a well-traveled road. Well known to the Apache Indians, this gold deposit was "discovered" by a party of white prospectors during the nineteenth century. Over the years, the site yielded millions of dollars worth of gold, all panned from the little stream that flows through the canyon. Since the mid-1980s, a few knowledgeable weekend gold panners have also regularly harvested nuggets from this stream.

The deposit, known as the Lost Adams Diggings, was named after a man who was a significant part of an expedition in 1864. That a fortune in gold nuggets was taken from the stream by Adams and his partners cannot be doubted. A short time later, however, the canyon was abandoned, the miners slaughtered or run off by Apache Indians. Adams made several attempts to return years later but was never successful. Since then, the exact location has been in dispute, earning the deposit the appellation "lost." Several have insisted they found the Lost Adams Diggings, but their claims never held up under investigation. Others arrived at the right location, occasionally found gold, but were not aware of the story of Adams and his legendary lost placer mine.

The tale of the Lost Adams Diggings is one of the best known in America. It was popularized first by Dobie in his book *Apache Gold and Yaqui Silver* in 1928 and more recently in my own *Buried Treasures of the American Southwest*, *New Mexico Treasure Tales*, and *Lost Mines and Buried Treasures of Arizona*. It is one of the strongest and most mythologized tales of lost treasure on the continent. A number of its features, geographical and cultural, have been verified, though for a century and a half, the exact location was in dispute.

Adams, the man credited with leading the party that arrived at the placer deposit and for whom it was named, was a real person. People who knew him were interviewed. Adams was still alive, in fact, when the elusive diggings achieved the status of legend.

Gold was taken from Adams's canyon in enormous quantities, with nuggets as small as a dust particle to as large as a hen's egg, all plucked from the bottom of a shallow stream. The gold was sometimes harvested by the Apache Indians, who used it to trade for rifles and ammunition, and then later by Adams and his party of miners. In more recent times, gold was taken from the stream by laborers hired to build the highway that passes near the mouth of the canyon. Road construction was halted for a time when work crews left the job to pan for gold.

Gold still exists there. I have seen it, handled it. I have watched patient gold panners fill soup cans and cola bottles with an inch or two of nuggets over an afternoon's work. Riches can be obtained, but there are challenges and risks associated with the quest. In recent years, the entrance to the canyon has been fenced off by a prominent mining corporation that is heavily invested in a large-scale gold-harvesting operation. Signs on the fence every few dozen yards warn that trespassers will be prosecuted. The source of the gold is the same geological formation in which Adams and his party found the abundant ore. During a recent visit, I witnessed armed security guards patrolling the area every fifteen minutes.

Should one obtain entrance to the canyon, dangers can be encountered in the form of rattlesnakes, which are abundant during the warmer months. With almost every turn of a rock, one encounters scorpions. Poisonous centipedes are common and can inflict painful wounds to the unsuspecting and unwary. The canyon is also home to black bears and mountain lions.

There is an additional element in this mix, a curious one and one difficult to explain. Perhaps it portends potential danger, perhaps not. The canyon appears to be watched over by men referred to as sentinels. During the earliest visits to the canyon by white men, they reported being observed by Indians who stationed themselves at or near the ridge tops. This canyon has long been sacred to Apaches, who lived and hunted in the region for generations, but evidence has surfaced that the locale may once have been homeland to the Aztecs, an advanced and powerful civilization that ruled vast portions of Mexico far to the south. History tells us that the Aztecs lived and thrived in the region of the southwestern United States before venturing into Mexico. After establishing their culture hundreds of miles away, they continued to return to that region to harvest gold and turquoise as well as other minerals and stones. It is likely they plucked gold nuggets from this same stream. During a recent expedition to the canyon, a weathered yet distinct pictographic image of a shaman was discovered in the same area the Apaches declared sacred. This suggests the site was regarded as holy perhaps as much as five thousand years prior to the arrival of the Apaches. The image was similar to ones found as far away as the Pecos River valley of West Texas, the mountains of Utah, and near the coast of California.

According to visitors to the canyon since the time when Adams and his partners lived there, the sentinels continue to watch over the region. They have been spotted against the backdrop of the sky along the ridges, sometimes unmoving, sometimes disappearing only to reappear at another location. According to legend and at least one eyewitness, the sentinels who patrol the canyon of gold today are descendants of the Indians, but the exact tribe with which they are associated is unclear.

Because of the allure of gold and the promise of wealth, the Lost Adams Diggings has been searched for by thousands of hopeful prospectors and adventurers during the past 150 years. Dozens have claimed discovery, but their declarations have never held up under investigation; nor did the finders ever return home with any significant amount of gold. There have been many seekers of the Lost Adams Diggings, but most, if not all, operated on misinformation and/or misinterpretation of reported experience and clues. The reason these numerous claims are not valid is because the searchers were, for the most part, never within two hundred miles of the lost canyon. I know, because I have been there, and it is not where Dobie and dozens of others claimed it could be found.

As a treasure-recovery professional, I have had numerous opportunities over the years to participate in various stages, from planning to recovery, of one expedition after another in search of the Lost Adams Diggings. What I have learned is that the organizers of these expeditions invariably misinterpreted or misunderstood the stated and long-accepted distances and directions left by Adams, information that was subsequently repeated, reinterpreted, and misinterpreted by others. They confused or misidentified landmarks and misread the geology and geography of the region. In the end they found nothing because they were all searching in a region nowhere close to the actual canyon of gold.

In 1990, the canyon and the gold were rediscovered and positively identified as a result of an odd set of circumstances involving a disabled former truck driver named Jim Peterson. His story is an amazing one and, at first, difficult to believe. During early conversations with Peterson, I expressed my own doubts about his claim of discovery. He responded by taking me to the canyon, guiding me through the area, pointing out all the significant geographic landmarks and other identifiable features, down to the most minute detail. By the time he was finished, I was convinced that I was at last standing on the bank of the gold-filled stream in Adams's lost canyon, a stream from which a king's ransom was once harvested. Subsequent visits to the canyon to verify distance, direction, and landmarks left no room for doubt.

As I stood alongside Peterson pondering my experience, I glanced up at the nearby ridge tops. Seventy-five yards away and standing next to a tall juniper was a man looking down at us, unmoving. His desert-brown skin was dark in the shadow of a tree. He was trim and sported a headband that secured a long mane of straight black hair that fell below his shoulders. The man was watching us. I turned to say something to Peterson, and when I looked back, the sentinel was gone.

What follows is the true story of the Lost Adams Diggings, starting at the beginning when Adams was first informed of the rich deposit of gold in a remote mountain range and ending with the story of my own search and discovery. I will provide sufficient detail to show that the long-sought location was nowhere near where most researchers and treasure hunters believed it to be. In addition, I will reinterpret the existing information in a logical and lucid manner in an effort to show how it leads directly to the true location of the Lost Adams Diggings, where a fortune in placer gold can be harvested.

PART I

The Story

✢ 1 ✢

The Man Called Adams

The man history associates most closely with what may have been, and perhaps still is, the richest placer gold mine in the Northern Hemisphere was known only as Adams. No verifiable first name has ever been attributed to him, and no photograph of Adams has ever been found.

Adams was a somewhat enigmatic, elusive, and sometimes reclusive figure during the 1860s and 1870s, showing up in public only during attempts to relocate the famous gold mine that still bears his name. Even today, little is known about Adams, his family, or where he came from. Ask any professional treasure hunter or those intimate with America's most famous tales of lost mines about Adams's diggings, however, and they will know most of the details of his discovery.

Adams once told an interviewer that he was born in Rochester, New York, on July 10, 1829, but revealed nothing of his background. According to the few who knew him, Adams may have lied about his origins. This is not unusual, as during the nineteenth century many newcomers to the American West who had left behind questionable pasts chose to establish new lives accompanied by different names. Some have suggested Adams might have been an outlaw from the east who fled the hangman's noose, but nothing has ever surfaced to suggest this was anything but a fabrication. Others insist he came from Oregon, where he was a failed gold miner and entrepreneur, and a few documents exist that strongly suggest a connection between Adams and that state. Whatever the truth, it is likely lost forever in the maze and mire of history.

What is known to be true of Adams, in addition to his association with the famous lost canyon of gold, is that he worked for a freight company transporting goods from Los Angeles, California, to Tucson, Arizona, and back. Adams hired on as a driver in 1861 while living in Los Angeles, and from what can be learned, he was a competent employee, was loyal to the company, and went about his duties without complaint.

One day in August 1864, Adams completed delivery of a load of freight in Tucson and collected the $2,000 payment from the customer. From there, he proceeded to another location in the city and loaded his wagon with merchandise to be transported back to Los Angeles. For a few days Adams dallied in Tucson, enjoying the pleasures of restaurant-cooked meals and drams of whiskey to wash away the dust of the trail. A short time later he was back on the road, heading west toward California, his wagon and trailer piled high with goods and pulled by a team of six stout draft horses. Behind him trailed a string of twelve riding horses, part of his delivery consignment.

Approximately one week and 120 miles later, Adams pulled off the main road and set up camp for the evening a short distance from the tiny but growing settlement of Gila Bend northwest of Tucson. During this part of his journey, he claimed, he passed by a Pima Indian village called Sacaton. He unhitched the draft animals, checked their hooves, and led them over to a nearby patch of grass. As was his practice when transporting consignment horses, he turned the animals out to graze. Here, he was fortunate to find lush grasses growing on the wide, flat, fertile flood plain of the Gila River. Weary from the journey, Adams decided not to go to the effort of hobbling the animals, believing they would be fine on their own and not stray too far. This proved to be a mistake.

Adams prepared his evening meal over a campfire, ate while he leaned against one wheel of the wagon, rinsed his plate and pot in the river, and returned them to the equipment box. After a final check on the horses grazing nearby, he crawled into his bedroll and fell asleep on the ground underneath the vehicle.

Sometime during the night, Adams was awakened by the sound of galloping horses. Climbing out of his bedroll, he scurried out from under the wagon in time to spot a half dozen young Apaches driving the horses southwestward in the direction of the Sauceda Mountains. The Indians herded the animals at full gallop and had disappeared over a low rise by the time Adams had pulled on his boots.

Cursing, Adams buckled on his gun belt and grabbed his rifle from the bed of the wagon. After levering a round into the chamber, he set out on foot after the horse thieves, hopeful of catching up with them. He was certain they would stop to rest the animals a few miles away.

Much to Adams's surprise, he overtook the Indians and the stolen horses only two miles from the campsite. The young rustlers had stopped in a shallow arroyo to give the animals a blow. As the Apaches admired the newly captured mounts, they were unaware of Adams's silent approach along the back of the arroyo. When he was close enough to pick out his targets in the lessening dark of early morning, he fired into their midst, killing two of them. The remaining Indians panicked and fled, leaving the eighteen horses behind.

It took Adams two hours to gather all the animals; most of them, spooked from the gunfire, had dashed out of the low arroyo and onto the adjacent flats. The sun had been up for over an hour by the time he had gathered his stock and began herding it back toward the campsite.

When Adams was still a half mile away, he spotted a plume of smoke rising from the location where he had left the wagon and trailer. Quickening his pace, he arrived at the campsite to discover the vehicles ablaze. The harnesses and other leather tack had been cut to pieces and strewn along the ground. As he walked around the burning wagon and trailer, Adams saw that most of the goods he was transporting had been taken. The items left behind had either been burned or tossed into the nearby brush. The $2,000 in cash he carried in a pouch stashed behind the wagon seat was nowhere to be found. Adams realized that the theft of the horses was a diversion designed to lure him from the camp so the wagons could be looted.

Riding one of the draft horses bareback and herding the rest, Adams set out for a Pima Indian village a few miles to the east, the one he claimed he had passed the previous day. All he possessed were the clothes he wore and his rifle and pistol. At the village, he hoped to trade one or more of the animals for enough supplies to get back to California.

It was late afternoon when, about a mile from the Pima village, Adams spotted a group of twenty men panning for gold in a narrow stream that flowed into the Gila River. He stopped to visit with them and to let the horses rest, water, and graze.

The miners told Adams they were from Pennsylvania and Ohio and on their way to what they were told were promising gold fields in the Sierra Nevada Mountains of California. They were nearly out of funds when a member of the party found a small amount of gold flake in the little stream next to which they were camped. Hoping to pan enough gold to purchase supplies for the remainder of their journey, the optimistic miners decided to remain for a few days. Less than half of them owned horses. The rest traveled on foot and had to carry their supplies and equipment on their backs. Naturally, they were interested in obtaining Adams's mounts and undertook to bargain with him, offering some of their gold as payment. Adams explained that the horses did not belong to him but promised to think about it. He was enjoying the company of the miners and told them he would discuss the possibility of a trade the next morning. For now, he said, he just wanted to rest.

2

Gotch Ear and the Tale of Apache Gold

That evening, as Adams sat by his campfire and watched the miners panning in the small stream, he spotted a rider coming from the direction of the Pima village. Without speaking, the newcomer rode to a spot close to Adams and sat silently atop his pony, also contemplating the miners. Adams noted that the man was young, probably no more than twenty, and dressed in the manner of the Apache. On the right side of his head, he sported a deformed ear that resembled a piece of knotted rope. Sensing the newcomer's friendliness, Adams invited him over to his campfire to share his coffee.

During their subsequent conversation, Adams learned that the young man was neither Apache nor Pima but Mexican. In broken English, he explained to Adams that, as young children, he and his brother were taken by the Apaches during a raid on the family rancho located somewhere deep in the Mexican state of Sonora in the foothills of the Sierra Madres. The two boys lived with the Indians for years and learned their language and ways. During the past several months, he said, the tribe had camped near the Santa Rosa Mountains, a few days' ride to the southeast. While there, the brother was killed by one of the Apaches during an argument. In retaliation, the young man with the deformed ear had slain his brother's killer.

The Apaches were angered not only that one of their own was killed but that the slayer had not complied with the formal system of tribal justice and sought recourse via the elders. Fearing retribution, he stole a horse that same night, fled the Indian camp, and rode away toward the northwest. He had arrived at the Pima village only a few days before Adams rode in. Because of his twisted ear, the Pima had given him a name that translated to "Gotch Ear."

That evening, Gotch Ear stretched out on the ground to sleep about twenty yards from Adams. In the morning, the two drank more coffee and sat together watching the miners work in the sandy bed of the shallow stream. Adams noted that each time one of the miners grew excited about retrieving a tiny amount of gold, Gotch Ear reacted with amusement and scorn. When Adams asked him why, Gotch Ear said such a small amount of gold was little reason for jubilance. After several seconds of silence, he turned to Adams and told him that there was a canyon located ten days' ride to the east where so much gold could be gathered from the stream in a single day that a stout burro would have difficulty transporting it. The nuggets, he said, were as big as acorns. In the rocks near where the stream originated, he continued, there was a seam of gold out of which chunks as large as turkey eggs could be pried. Gotch Ear gestured vaguely eastward and told Adams that the canyon was difficult to find. Worse, he said, it was located in the land of the Apaches, who regarded it as a sacred place.

Adams asked the young man how he had come to know about this amazing canyon containing such a wealth in gold nuggets. Gotch Ear explained that when he and his brother were living with an Apache band led by Chief Nana, the tribe visited the canyon many times. He said he had seen hundreds of gold nuggets as large as wild grapes lying beneath the clear waters of the shallow stream that wound its way through the canyon. It was an easy thing, he said, to reach into the stream and pluck out the gold with one's fingers.

Adams asked Gotch Ear why the Apaches did not harvest this plentiful gold. The young man said that the Indians had little use for the mineral. Sometimes it was hammered out and shaped into ornaments, but Apaches generally cared little for such things. Now and then, a quantity of the gold would be harvested to trade for rifles and ammunition, but for the most part it was left alone. According to author J. Frank Dobie, Gotch Ear told Adams the canyon was revered as a sacred place and had been guarded by Indian sentinels since the beginning of time. It was an area best left undisturbed. When white miners or travelers had entered the canyon in the past, they were killed, scalped, and mutilated by the warriors of Chief Nana's band. Gotch Ear said he had witnessed the torture and murder of several miners and prospectors.

Dobie also credited Gotch Ear with providing the name of the canyon: Sno-ta-hay. Research has revealed no such word exists in the Apache language. The word that comes closest, according to Paul Ortega, a Mescalero Apache, is Itsnatahey, which means "too close dark mountains." This term seems logical and appropriate for the region and will be used throughout the rest of this book. It is reasonable to assume that the spelling mistake made by Dobie and others was simply the result of the way they thought the word was pronounced and written.

Undeterred by tales of murderous Indians, Adams asked Gotch Ear if he could lead a party of men to Itsnatahey Canyon. The Mexican agreed that he could. When Adams inquired about Chief Nana and the likelihood of encountering him, Gotch Ear speculated that if the chief was in a good mood he might allow men to pan for the gold. On the other hand, he said, the Indian leader might decide to kill them.

Later that day, Adams repeated Gotch Ear's story of the fabulous canyon of gold to some of the miners. All reacted with excitement about the prospect of finding such great wealth in the remote canyon, a promise that sounded infinitely better than what might await them in California. When Adams told the miners about the possibility of encountering hostile Apaches, they replied that they were all well armed with rifles and revolvers and could likely hold their own against an Indian war party. To the last man, they urged Adams to negotiate a deal with Gotch Ear to lead them to the gold.

When Adams communicated the interests and intentions of the miners to Gotch Ear, the Mexican shrugged and said he would take them to the canyon in exchange for two good horses, a saddle, a rifle, some ammunition, and two fifty-dollar gold pieces, all of which represented impressive wealth to the Apache-raised young man. Gotch Ear told Adams that, if after a certain amount of time deemed reasonable by the miners he had not led them to the canyon where they would find large gold nuggets in abundance, he would allow himself to be stood against a rock and shot dead.

At dawn on July 20, 1864, Adams and the twenty miners responded to the call to adventure and wealth. Led by Gotch Ear, they rode and walked out of their campsite near the Pima village and into history and folklore.

⁂ 3 ⁂

The Journey

The journey to the canyon of gold was long, slow, tedious, and often difficult. The party encountered not a single white settlement along the way and only a few Indian encampments. In fact, they encountered no white men at all. During the trip, Adams attempted to make mental notes of landmarks, but, as he demonstrated often during this and subsequent trips, he was not one for detail and, by his own admission, possessed a poor sense of distance and direction. Adams was unable to remember much about the country he passed through, and his inability to recall important landmarks and the various locations and orientations of the trails traveled would plague him for the rest of his life.

It is generally agreed among most researchers that the route followed by Gotch Ear led variously eastward and northeastward. This conclusion was derived from interviews with Adams wherein he stated the party traveled for the most part in a northeastward direction, though in later years he admitted to some uncertainty. Until recent years, these original directions and descriptions were taken at face value, with no attempt at any kind of logical investigation and reconstruction. Adams also stated that several days after commencing the trip, the party passed between what he identified as Mount Ord and Mount Thomas in eastern Arizona. As he had never been in that part of the country, it is difficult to understand how he would know of those mountains or their names.

Most professional treasure-recovery specialists who have studied Adams's tale of the great gold discovery are convinced that he erred in his identifications of these landforms since, as learned in later years, the Gotch Ear–led party was, for the most part, nowhere near the route that Adams initially claimed he had traveled.

Adams also maintained that he and the group passed by the White Mountains and crossed what he described as two large rivers he identified as the Black and the Little Colorado. How Adams kenned any of this remains a mystery. On another occasion, years later, Adams insisted they crossed the San Francisco River. Note that the San Francisco River is due east of Gila Bend and not far from the town of Clifton, near the border with New Mexico. This location will surface again relative to the determination of the precise geographic location of the gold-filled stream.

After fording the last of the two major rivers, assumed by many to be the Black and the Little Colorado, Adams claimed they crossed a well-traveled wagon road that Gotch Ear told them led to Fort Wingate, located many miles to the north and east and near the present-day town of Gallup, New Mexico.

The ten days necessary to reach the canyon of gold estimated by Gotch Ear turned into fourteen. Unlike Indians, who travel swift and light, the white men, unused to the rugged country and bearing heavy packs, took longer. Late one evening after fourteen days of travel, according to Adams, Gotch Ear guided the party to a good campsite located at the southern entrance to a large canyon and a short distance from a spring out of which flowed cool, fresh water. Years later, Adams contradicted himself and insisted the party arrived at this location after only eight days of travel, an unlikely achievement given the remoteness of the area and the rugged, roadless terrain. The next morning, Gotch Ear told Adams that they were now only a short distance from Itsnatahey, the canyon of gold. He repeated his warning that this was the land of the feared Apache chief Nana and that the Indians often camped in the very canyon they were about to enter.

Gotch Ear repeated frightening tales of the Indians slaying miners and others who entered the canyon, as well as occasional travelers who had chanced along the same trail they were following. Now that they were so close to their destination and far from any succor whatsoever, the miners grew troubled and uneasy. Time and again they checked to make certain their rifles and handguns were clean and loaded. They cast frightened glances about the nearby encircling ridges and peered intently into the thick forests of pine and spruce. One particularly anxious member of the party, a German, was apparently unused to the rigors of rough travel and the dangers of the wilderness. Time and again he insisted Adams do something to guarantee his safety.

The next morning, as the miners ate breakfast, Gotch Ear informed them that a short distance ahead they would encounter a pumpkin patch irrigated and cultivated by Apache women using water from the same spring from which they had just filled their canteens. In addition to the pumpkins, he said, they would find corn and squash.

After cleaning their breakfast pans and dishes and repacking their supplies and gear onto the horses, the miners followed Gotch Ear out of the camp and up the trail into the canyon. The ride was slow and difficult due to the rough and rocky terrain. Adams claimed that, in places, the canyon walls pinched in so tight it was possible for a rider on horseback to extend his arms and touch the rock on both sides.

During the ride into the canyon, Adams was concerned that it offered an ideal place for an ambush since they could only advance slowly. Furthermore, the extremely narrow canyon, said Adams, would have made turning the horses to retreat almost impossible, should it become necessary. Nervous, Adams scanned the tops of the canyon walls. He had a feeling they were being watched. He also had a premonition that in the days ahead they would encounter threats and danger.

✢ 4 ✢

The Canyon of Gold

Around mid-morning of the following day, after traveling less than two miles over a trail thick with rough cobbles and large rocks, the party arrived at the pumpkin patch. There, a narrow floodplain of the creek bottom had been cultivated and showed evidence of pumpkins and other vegetables. After traveling a bit farther, Gotch Ear pointed toward the northeast to two mountains. Referring to them as the Piloncillos, the Mexican stated that they were located just beyond the canyon of gold. *Piloncillo* is a Spanish word for "sugar cone," which the two peaks indeed resembled.

According to the account provided by J. Frank Dobie, Gotch Ear led the miners across the creek to the east wall of the canyon. There, partially concealed by a large boulder, he pointed to a narrow opening. After pausing for several minutes and scanning the nearby forest and ridge tops as though looking and listening for something, Gotch Ear rode through the opening, beckoning the miners to follow.

Trailing Gotch Ear through the constricted entrance, Adams and the other members of the party proceeded along a gently sloping trail littered with boulders, large and small, which made travel difficult. Adams later described much of the canyon as Z-shaped, with a narrow, shallow creek trickling down the middle. From time to time the trail crossed the little stream.

After a period of slow and tortuous progress, the canyon widened somewhat into a small valley filled with pine, juniper, and oak trees. The creek they were following bubbled and sang as it flowed over rocks along its course. The riders paused long enough to water their horses. Some of the men dismounted to take a drink or to relieve themselves. Not far from where they had stopped, the canyon opened into a bit of clearing. To Adams, it looked like a suitable place to set up a campsite.

Three hundred yards farther upstream and around a bend, explained Gotch Ear, was a twelve-foot-high waterfall. Beyond the waterfall, the canyon continued sloping upward toward a distant ridge. From this ridge, the two rounded mountaintops spotted earlier could be seen in the distance.

Making their way over to the clearing, the rest of the miners dismounted and regarded the valley they had entered. The horses were left to drink the clear water from the stream and graze on the grasses that grew there. When one of the miners asked how long it would be before they arrived at the place where they would find gold, Gotch Ear pointed to the slow-moving creek. Though exhausted from the difficult travel, several of the miners searched through their packs, retrieved gold pans, and knelt along the banks. They scooped sand, gravel, and water from the creek into the pans and swirled the slurry around.

Within seconds, excited shouts from the men echoed against the canyon walls as they picked gold nuggets from the pans. More minutes passed, and the miners were soon whooping with delight as they displayed marble-sized pieces of the precious ore to one another, comparing the size, quantity, and quality of the nuggets. All thoughts of seeing to the horses, preparing dinner, and setting up shelters for the night vanished as the men bent to harvest the immeasurable wealth.

Only Adams remained standing on the bank of the stream, peering into the upper reaches of the canyon and wondering if they were being observed by Apache sentinels who might have been roused by the shouts of the ecstatic miners.

The next two days found the party still hard at work panning gold. They barely took time to eat, and when they did, they paused only long enough to down some of the remaining hardtack and jerky they carried. With the exception of Adams and Gotch Ear, none of the party took the time to build a fire to make coffee or prepare a meal. When they became so tired they could no longer hold a gold pan, they simply lay down on the bare rocks next to the stream or under a nearby tree and caught what sleep they needed. After a few hours of rest, they were back at work.

At the end of the second day, Gotch Ear approached Adams and told him he was ready to leave. Adams told the Mexican he could pick out any two horses he wanted from the string of twenty-six and help himself to one of the few saddles available. Adams presented Gotch Ear with his own rifle and all the ammunition he had remaining in his pouch, along with two fifty-dollar gold pieces contributed by the miners. Happy with the trade, Gotch Ear waved good-bye as he rode out of the canyon. Months later, Adams would learn that two of Chief Nana's warriors had been seen riding the same horses and that one of them was carrying the rifle he had given to Gotch Ear.

During the next few days, as more gold accumulated, Adams, with encouragement from the miners, fell into the role of official leader of the party. At his suggestion, it was agreed that all the gold would be placed in canvas pouches, stored in a common location, and divided equally at such time as they decided to leave the canyon. Only one man refused to participate in the arrangement. The German, supposedly named Emil Schaeffer and called the "Dutchman" by the others, preferred working alone, eschewing the camaraderie of the other men.

While panning gold from the stream, one or another of the miners would occasionally look up to see two or more Indians standing atop a nearby ridge watching the activities of the newcomers. At first, the sight of the Indians frightened the miners, but as no attempt was made to approach or attack, they eventually relaxed and continued with their work. Adams was informed about the sentinels, and he kept a cautious eye on the ridges and a loaded rifle close by.

Given the communal arrangement, because the party was getting low on meat, Adams assigned some of the men to hunt the abundant deer, turkey, and other wild game found in the canyon. The fresh meat was appreciated by all, and a quantity of venison was smoked over a low fire as the miners worked.

Since winter was nearing, shelter became necessary. A team of men was assigned to cut down trees and used some of the horses to drag the skinned and trimmed logs to the center of the small clearing. Other men notched the logs, and soon the construction of a cabin was underway. The structure was relatively compact, measuring sixteen by eighteen feet and consisting of only one room where all the miners slept. At one end, a rock hearth and chimney were constructed. Next to the hearth, according to Adams, a chamber was excavated and lined with stones. Into this cavity they placed the sacks of accumulated gold. The amount of precious metal grew at a fast rate, and Adams was convinced the cavity would soon be filled.

As the days passed and the men continued to pan the stream, the miners continued to spot one or two Indians at a time watching them from the ridges. Adams identified the Indians as Apaches. Though the miners remained cautious and nervous as a result of the sentinels, they soon grew used to the sight.

And then, the Indians came.

✤ 5 ✤

Chief Nana

When the log cabin was nearly completed, the miners were surprised by a visit from Chief Nana and a group of two dozen mounted, painted, and armed warriors. Nana was head of the Chihenne Band, better known as Warm Springs Apaches. His real name was Kaz-Tziden, which meant "broken foot." The name Nana, given to him by the Mexicans, translates to "grandma." Nana, born in 1800, was sixty-four years old when he confronted Adams in the canyon. The Apache chief ultimately lived to be ninety-six. Some historians claim Nana led a band of one hundred warriors, but the number was probably closer to forty.

With menacing visage, Nana rode directly up to Adams and demanded an explanation for why this contingent of white men was digging in the stream that ran through Itsnatahey Canyon, the sacred gathering place of the Apaches.

Adams explained to Nana that the men only wished to pan for some of the gold found there and represented no threat to the Indians whatsoever. When they had accumulated a sufficient amount of the ore, he explained, they would depart from the canyon as they had come, quietly and with respect.

Nana pondered this response for several minutes. He acknowledged that the gold was of little use to the Apaches. He agreed to allow the miners to remain as long as they promised to respect the valley and the water. The chief also cautioned Adams not to allow his men to overhunt the wild game in the valley, as it was important to the Apaches who lived there. Adams agreed that it would be as the chief instructed.

Growing stern, Nana then issued a warning. Pointing upstream, he said that the white men must not pass into the upper part of Itsnatahey Canyon beyond the waterfall. That area, he said, was holy, and the Apaches camped there. It was not to be profaned by the presence of outsiders. If a single miner violated this restriction, said Nana, all would be killed.

Adams calmly explained to the chief that all the gold they could possibly want could be found in this lower portion of the canyon well below the waterfall and that none of them had any reason to visit the region sacred to the Apaches.

With that, Nana wheeled his mount around and rode back up the canyon, followed by his warriors. Silence reigned in the camp for several minutes as the miners pondered the Apache chief's warning. Then, anxious to increase their rapidly growing wealth, they returned to the business of panning gold. Adams, along with two volunteers, continued with the construction of the cabin.

More weeks passed, and the space next to the hearth was growing full with pouches of gold nuggets. Adams estimated the cavity held almost $100,000 worth of the ore, an impressive fortune in 1864. While the hunters kept the party supplied with fresh meat, the miners had run disastrously low on supplies such as flour, coffee, sugar, tinned goods, hard candy, and cornmeal. The horses had grazed almost all of the grass available in the clearing as well as some distance up and down the stream. Feed and grain for the animals would also be required. Aware of the need to obtain such items, according to the J. Frank Dobie version of the tale, Adams selected a contingent of eight men to ride to the nearest settlement or military post to purchase food, ammunition, some tools, and other supplies. A miner named John Brewer was placed in charge of the expedition.

✢ 6 ✢

The Brewer Expedition

Most of what people know, or think they know, of the John Brewer–led expedition to obtain supplies and the sequence of events that followed his departure derives from the account presented by author J. Frank Dobie in *Apache Gold and Yaqui Silver*. Others who have written about the Lost Adams Diggings have included this episode, but their versions repeat Dobie's treatment with no effort to determine details. John Brewer's version of what happened, as told by A. M. Tenny Jr. in 1928, differs significantly from the Dobie story (see chapter 10).

According to Dobie, as John Brewer and his party prepared for the journey to the nearest point of supply, the German stepped forward and told Adams he wished to leave the canyon and would ride out with the others. Adams told him he was free to do so. Within minutes, the German was packed and ready to go. Each member of the party rode a horse. Six additional horses were taken along to transport the supplies. Only nine horses remained in camp. Brewer was given a quantity of gold from the large cache to pay for the provisions. Adams estimated it would take a total of eight days to reach a settlement, purchase the supplies, and return. As the group rode away, Adams was concerned that the twelve men left in camp might not be sufficient to repel an attack by the Apaches.

While awaiting the return of their companions, the remaining miners continued panning the gold. Each expressed amazement that there appeared to be no end to the riches they could glean from the gravels of the small stream. Adams estimated that each of the men in the party was now wealthy beyond his wildest imagination. At night around the fire, the miners took turns talking about what they would do with their share of the gold when they returned to civilization. Most talked of going back to their families, selling their farms or businesses, and leading a life of luxury somewhere they had always dreamed of residing. Others spoke of the fine clothes and shoes and horses and carriages such wealth would purchase. Some talked of starting new businesses and elevating their social status. Still others thought about traveling to exotic, faraway places. Adams thought he might use his share to start his own freight company. As the days passed, the miners noticed that the number of sentinels watching them from the ridge tops was increasing.

On the fourth day after the Brewer-led party departed, one of the miners showed Adams a gold nugget the leader described years later as "large as a hen's egg." Stunned at the magnificent piece of ore, Adams asked where it had come from. To his surprise and dismay, the miner related that he had trailed after two stray horses to a point above the waterfall. While there, he noticed several large gold nuggets lying at the bottom of the stream.

Fearful of the consequences should any of the miners be caught in the forbidden location, Adams reminded the man of the warning leveled at all of them by Chief Nana and cautioned him against returning to the area.

Unable to keep his amazing discovery to himself, the miner who found the large nugget informed the others. That same night, five of the men, lured by even greater wealth than they already possessed, crept out of the camp, followed the stream to a location several yards above the waterfall, and proceeded to harvest quantities of large gold pieces from the gravels. The following morning, the same five men approached Adams and showed him a coffeepot filled with the huge nuggets. Once again, the leader reminded them of Chief Nana's warning and insisted they never return to that location, admonishing that they were placing the lives of all the men in jeopardy. When the five miners showed the other members of the party the collection of gold nuggets, however, they scrambled madly to reach the area above the falls. Their greed proved their undoing.

✤ 7 ✤

Massacre

At the end of the eighth day, Brewer and his men had not re-turned, and Adams grew worried. Not only was there now an acute shortage of supplies, but he feared that some disaster might have befallen the party. Adams hoped and prayed that was not the case. If the men did not return by mid-morning of the following day, Adams decided, he would take one of the miners and go in search of them.

By noon of the next day the Brewer party had not returned. Adams, concerned, decided to ride out to the opening of the canyon and wait for the miners. He selected Jack Davidson to accompany him. They saddled two of the horses and rode down the canyon in hopes of meeting their returning companions. Years later, Adams confessed to harboring a sinking feeling during the ride that something awful had occurred.

When Adams and Davidson reached the narrow opening to Itsnatahey Canyon, their worst fears were realized. Lying scattered across the ground near the entrance were the dead, scalped, and freshly mutilated remains of what Adams estimated to be at least five of his friends. All of the horses were gone, presumably taken by the Indians. Littering the rocky ground between what was left of the miners were remnants of the newly purchased supplies, at least what the Indians had not carried away. Adams spotted an Apache arrow piercing the torso of one of the victims. He fervently hoped that the three missing miners had escaped. Adams deduced that the party had reached this point during their return trip when they were spotted by sentinels, attacked, and slaughtered. Adams was convinced this was retaliation for the trespass into the realm of the sacred canyon that had been forbidden to the party.

Adams and Davidson walked among the dismembered bodies of the miners to salvage food and other items left on the ground. The two men wanted to bury the bodies, but they had no shovels and the ground was far too rocky. Instead, they gathered up the remains and placed them under a nearby shallow rock overhang that afforded some protection against the elements.

Concerned that the rest of the miners might be in grave danger, Adams hastened to return to the camp and explain the fate of the supply party. He planned to insist that they gather the accumulated gold, each man carrying as much as he could, and then depart the canyon with all haste. It was just a matter of time, reasoned Adams, before Nana and his warriors raided the camp. As he spurred his mount back up the canyon, Adams did not realize he was already too late.

Evening was approaching as Adams and Davidson made their way back toward the camp. On nearing the clearing with the cabin, the two men heard gunshots, the shrill war cries of the Apaches, and the screams of their dying comrades. Dismounting, they stared in horror. Dozens of mounted warriors rode back and forth across the open area in front of the cabin, shooting, spearing, hacking, and scalping the hapless miners. As some of the Apaches went through the pockets of jackets and britches in search of valuables or useful items, others set the log cabin afire.

Dazed by the violence of what they were witnessing, as well as the growing blaze of the fire, Adams and Davidson stood in mute shock at the brutality that transpired. Adams regained his composure after a few minutes and, fearing discovery by the Indians, pulled Davidson into the cover of some low-growing bushes not far from the trail. From this point, the two men watched as the

Apaches fought over the miners' clothes, boots, scalps, and few remaining supplies. As darkness overtook the canyon, the Indians, carrying stolen weapons and other booty, mounted and rode upstream and beyond the waterfall.

Adams and Davidson waited for another hour until they were certain the last of the Apaches had gone. No sound could be heard, save for the gurgle of the stream trickling over rocks and an occasional crackle from the burning logs. Cautiously, the two men crawled out from under the bushes and crept toward what remained of the cabin. They intended to retrieve some of the gold hidden by the hearth and then leave the canyon. When they arrived at the still-burning structure, the intense heat prevented them from reaching the hidden chamber where the nuggets were cached.

Fearful that Apaches might return at any moment, Adams and Davidson retreated to where they had left the two horses. Finding them, they mounted up and rode down the narrow trail leading out of Itsnatahey. The only gold the men took out of the valley was a large nugget one of the miners had given Adams days earlier, a grape-sized lump of ore he carried in his shirt pocket.

⊹ 8 ⊹

Escape

After exiting the canyon, the two men spurred their mounts along the trail, out the narrow entrance, and past the pumpkin patch. They thought only of putting as much distance between them and Nana's Apaches as possible.

Several days later Adams and Davidson rode their tired horses westward across the Arizona desert. They carried neither food nor water. The two men had subsisted on acorns and piñon nuts until they left the forested mountains. Since then, they had eaten nothing. In desperation, they killed one of the horses, drank its blood, and dined on one of the haunches. They jerked more of the meat over a low fire, wrapped it in a blanket, and, riding double on the remaining horse, proceeded in a westerly direction in the hope of finding a ranch or a settlement.

Two weeks passed, and Adams and Davidson—emaciated, starving, and weak—encountered a platoon of US Cavalry. Years later, Adams stated that the soldiers were from Fort Apache. The two survivors were taken back to the military post and admitted to the hospital, where they were treated for exposure, exhaustion, and malnutrition.

According to Adams, the two were later transferred to Fort Whipple. There, he claimed, Davidson, who was in his fifties with a weak constitution, never recovered and died after a few days. At that point, said Adams, he was the sole survivor of the Itsnatahey

Canyon massacre and presumably the only white man who knew the location of the gold-nugget-filled cache near the cabin's hearth that contained the wealth of kings. Before he succumbed, Davidson allegedly told his doctor the story of the ill-fated expedition, his version varying little from Adams's.

Though Adams insisted the ordeal had led to Davidson's death, another account states that the partner not only survived but lived a relatively long life following his escape from the canyon. For years, according to interviews, Jack Davidson told and retold the story about the discovery of gold, the massacre, and the flight from the canyon across the desert. He claimed that during their escape, he and Adams rode through a mountain range he identified as the White Mountains of Arizona. Again, how Davidson, like Adams, would know such a thing about a region with which he was unfamiliar is a puzzle. Davidson verified Adams's claim that he was sent to Fort Whipple, where he could receive better treatment during his recovery.

In later years, Davidson was known as "Crazy Jack." It was said that he received a number of offers to guide parties of miners to the now famous lost canyon of gold but refused them all. He constantly warned others that the Indian sentinels would know of their arrival and alert others to their presence and that their lives would be in jeopardy.

In some ways, Adams himself never recovered from the experience in Itsnatahey Canyon. Physically stronger than Davidson, he soon regained his health and was free to move about the fort as he recuperated from his ordeal. His mind, however, had turned a corner and never found its way back to where it was before the incident in the canyon. Adams's sleep was filled with nightmares of Indian sentinels observing the activity of the miners, of Apaches attacking and killing his companions, of scalpings and mutilations.

Adams dreamed of the flaming log cabin and of the fortune of gold cached next to the stone hearth in the ashes of the burnt-down structure. He dreamed of the canvas pouches full of gold nuggets taken from the stream, gold that could make him a rich man, wealthier than any king.

While he was recuperating at Fort Apache, Adams spotted two young Apache Indians riding onto the post and recognized them as members of Chief Nana's band that had massacred his friends in Itsnatahey Canyon. He informed an officer but was told that as the Indians were serving as army scouts, nothing could be done. Enraged at the response, Adams stole a pistol from an inattentive corporal and used it to shoot and kill the two Apaches.

Adams was charged with murder and placed in the stockade to await trial. While incarcerated, he became friends with a young lieutenant who believed he had been justified in shooting the Indians. One night, the officer unlocked Adams's cell and allowed him to escape. Adams took a horse from one of the corrals and fled toward the southwest. Following a rugged journey across mountain ranges and hostile Indian country, he arrived in Tucson. There, he remained long enough to rest and recover. He sold the gold nugget he still carried for ninety-two dollars. With the money, he supplied himself with provisions to continue his journey westward. From Tucson, he traveled to Los Angeles, where he was eventually reunited with his wife and three children.

For the next ten years in California, Adams held a number of different jobs, including running a furniture store and operating a livery stable. He continued to suffer the same terrible nightmares in which he relived the ordeal of watching his friends die horribly at the hands of the marauding Apaches. Though he knew an uncountable fortune of gold awaited him in Itsnatahey Canyon, Adams could not convince himself to return for fear of encountering Chief Nana and his murderous warriors.

PART II
The Canyon Revisited

✤ 9 ✤

The Searchers

C. A. Shaw, a Canadian from Nova Scotia, was a retired ship captain who had amassed a comfortable fortune during his lifetime. Ever the entrepreneur, Shaw was always on the lookout for some business opportunity in which to invest. Shaw missed the challenge of the sea and spoiled for a good adventure from time to time. He found one when he learned the story of the Lost Adams Diggings.

During his travels around the United States, Shaw heard bits and pieces of the tale about the rich placer gold mine, the small stream in a remote canyon that yielded sizeable nuggets in great quantities. Many believed it was located somewhere in New Mexico; others thought it was in Arizona. Shaw learned of the tale from the physician who treated Adams at Fort Apache. He picked up other aspects of the story from soldiers who had known Adams briefly, and he heard yet another version from a trader who had done some business with the miner. Intrigued, Shaw set out in search of Adams, now forty-five years old, and located him at his home in Southern California. Shaw decided to make Adams an offer he couldn't refuse.

Shaw visited with Adams for hours about the canyon of gold, taking notes all the while. Shaw realized that as he spoke with the former freighter, Adams had difficulty recalling the geography of the region he and the miners had traveled through on their way to the canyon. Adams was uncertain, even unaware, of directions and distance. This concern would revisit Shaw time and again and cause serious problems between the two men.

Shaw explained to Adams that he was interested in financing an expedition to locate Itsnatahey Canyon and panning as much of the gold in the stream as possible. In addition, he would attempt to locate the hidden cache of nuggets near the hearth. Shaw explained to Adams that if he would serve as guide, he would be compensated handsomely and given a significant share of any gold found.

At first Adams refused, telling Shaw he wanted nothing to do with a return trip to the canyon. He described in detail the Indian attack and the horrible deaths of his friends at the hands of the Apaches. Shaw assured Adams that the US Army had removed the Indians from the region and placed them on reservations—there was nothing to fear. Adams insisted that the army was incapable of removing all the Apaches and that the sentinels would still be there, still watching from the adjacent ridge tops, still guarding the canyon against the intrusion of white men.

For the next several days, Shaw continued to visit with Adams at his home, all the while working hard to convince him to serve as expedition guide back to the canyon. Shaw agreed to recruit, equip, and arm sixteen qualified men to assist in the search. He repeated his offer of an impressive stipend if Adams consented to show them the way. Shaw explained over and over how all the members of the party would come away from the adventure very rich men. Finally, following a great deal of persuasion from Shaw, Adams reluctantly agreed.

Several weeks later, the expedition, consisting of Adams, Shaw, and sixteen men identified as miners and outdoorsmen, departed California and gathered at Gila Bend, Arizona. The men rendezvoused at the precise location where Adams had camped when the Apaches burned his wagon and goods. After allowing two days for the final preparations and giving their riding stock and pack horses time to rest, they set out to retrace the exact route traveled years earlier by the miners led by Gotch Ear. Abundant supplies and provisions were strapped to the backs of the pack-horses. Shaw had provided for any and all contingencies they might encounter—except one.

Shaw, aware that Adams had trouble remembering pertinent landmarks and routes and manifested considerable confusion when it came to distances and directions, worried constantly about whether they were following the correct route. The members of the expedition, however, were not prepared for what occurred on the very first day of travel. As a result of his inability to recall anything correctly, Adams got them lost.

Time and again, Adams was unable to recognize the landscape through which they passed. He could not recall any of the rivers and streams they crossed and became disoriented on a number of occasions. Adams's recollections of the original journey were vague and confused. Shaw and the men grew more and more frustrated and irritated by his inability to recall important information and wearied of the delays caused by his confusion.

"The Apaches made me forget," Adams told Shaw, but the truth was that Adams had always been challenged when it came to recalling anything pertinent about his travels. Following days of fruitless wandering, the failed expedition disbanded.

During the next ten years, Adams, sometimes with Shaw and sometimes on his own, attempted to organize and lead other expeditions in search of the lost canyon of gold. Like the first trip with Shaw, however, each subsequent adventure ended in failure. One Adams-led party searched for four months throughout a portion of northeastern Arizona and found no trace of anything resembling the canyon of gold. Upset with Adams, several members of the group threatened to hang him. Ultimately, they rode away and left him alone in the wilderness.

Three years following the disastrous expedition with Shaw, a man named Charles Clark was traveling around eastern Arizona searching for Adams's lost canyon of gold. Clark, an elderly man, had some mining experience but decided to invest his time in searching for the fabled canyon instead of laboring in a mineshaft. Clark had studied the various stories of the lost diggings he had heard in his travels and, coupled with what he knew of the geology and geography of eastern Arizona and western New Mexico, developed a theory about where the location might be. While Clark was certain he knew where the canyon could be found, his age and infirmity made traveling and living in the rugged outdoors difficult.

One night while Clark was camped outside of the town of Payson, Arizona, a stranger rode up and introduced himself as Edward S. Doheny. He told Clark he was traveling through the country looking for a job. The two men talked well into the night. By the next morning, Clark had grubstaked Doheny to follow his directions to the canyon, retrieve the gold cached near the stone hearth, and return. Weeks later, Doheny rode into Clark's camp and explained that he was never able to locate the canyon using the directions he had been given.

C. A. Shaw came back on the scene and organized more expeditions in search of the lost diggings, perhaps as many as twelve. Though he had little confidence in Adams's ability to find his way back to the canyon, Shaw occasionally employed him as a guide. By this time, most people had come to believe that Adams had lost his mind as a result of his horrible experience. Others were convinced he was merely incompetent. Shaw, however, maintained faith in Adams, believed his story, and insisted to all that his friend was honest and reliable. Shaw somehow convinced himself that Adams's lost canyon of gold was located somewhere in the Mogollon Mountains of western New Mexico and concentrated his searches in that area. Shaw regaled others with stories of his expeditions in search of the Lost Adams Diggings in the Mogollons, and over the next several years this range came to be closely associated with the mine.

Despite the misadventures that occurred when Adams was involved with the expeditions, Shaw had several experiences that convinced him that his friend was telling the truth. On one occasion he encountered an army post trader who claimed to have been at Fort Wingate in 1864. The trader recalled that a party of eight men had arrived to purchase supplies and paid with large gold nuggets. Just before departing, the men said they were miners and were returning to their rich placer mine. They pointed toward a distant location that was, according to the trader, south-southwest of the fort. Shaw was convinced this must have been the ill-fated Brewer party.

On another occasion, when Shaw and Adams were together at Fort Apache during one of the searches, a soldier identified Adams as the man who had stolen a lieutenant's horse and escaped from the stockade while awaiting trial for killing two Indian scouts.

Shaw eventually went through all of his savings as a result of funding failed expeditions in search of the lost diggings. When he ran out of his own money, he had some successes in raising funds from others. One of his backers was a man named Charles Allen. Allen sometimes accompanied Shaw and Adams on the expeditions throughout Arizona and New Mexico.

During the 1870s, according to Allen, Shaw and Adams were hanging around the trading post at Fort Apache when they encountered a small band of Apaches on their way to Arizona's San Carlos Apache Indian Reservation between the town of Globe and the border with New Mexico. As the Indians rode by, Adams pointed out Chief Nana to Shaw. The two men followed the Apaches to their campsite, and Adams confronted Nana, asking him when he had last visited Itsnatahey Canyon. According to Shaw, Nana stared, unblinking and hostile, at Adams for a long time, then turned and walked away.

Shaw also learned that Nana, prior to being forced onto the Indian reservation, had been good friends with the Warm Springs Agency trader, a man named Chase. During a conversation with Chase, Nana told the trader that someday he might take him to a place with a lot of gold easily plucked from the gravels of a small stream with one's fingers. When the trader asked where this canyon was located, Nana pointed toward the east and said the name of it was Itsnatahey.

Though unsuccessful, Shaw continued to hunt for the lost diggings for most of the rest of his life. Having spent the bulk of his savings on a number of failed expeditions, Shaw had little money left and his backers pulled out. In his later years, when he was able to put together a small expedition, it consisted of no more than three or four men. During previous searches, Shaw had provided mounts, equipment, and supplies, but now the men who accompanied him were expected to provide for themselves and received no salary, only a guaranteed share of the gold should they find any. Success, however, continued to elude the determined and persistent Shaw.

When Shaw grew too old and infirm to ride the rugged trails any longer, he contented himself with sitting at home in his easy chair and telling the stories of his searches for the Lost Adams Diggings to any and all who cared to listen. He died on August 15, 1917.

During the period when Adams was being treated at Fort Apache, he related his experiences in Itsnatahey Canyon, as well as his nightmares, to the attending physician, Dr. Spurgeon. Adams even showed Spurgeon the large gold nugget he carried in his pocket and told him it came from the canyon. Recalling his patient's provocative stories years later, Dr. Spurgeon became keenly interested in locating the canyon of gold himself.

When Adams spoke to the doctor of his journey to the diggings with the miners and Gotch Ear, he offered directions and distances as best he could remember them. He also provided descriptions of the canyon, the cabin, and the narrow gold-filled stream. Using a pencil, he sketched a crude map and gave it to Spurgeon. The doctor wrote the information down in a small black notebook. When his tour of duty with the army was completed,

Spurgeon returned to his home in Toledo, Ohio, to practice medicine. His thoughts, however, remained with Adams's lost canyon of gold, and he constantly dreamed of the riches he was convinced were to be found there. Finally, he decided to use Adams's directions and map and go in search of the canyon himself.

Spurgeon recruited a number of men to accompany him, but neither the physician nor his companions, most of them business and professional men, were hardy or experienced enough for the rugged trails they were forced to travel and for the rigors of living in the mountainous environment.

The hardships of the trail proved too much for Spurgeon and his party. Before reaching the place the doctor believed to be the precise location of the canyon of gold, the expedition fell apart. Spurgeon despaired of ever finding the gold himself, but he told Adams's story to another man, John Dowling. In 1881, the physician enlisted the help of Dowling and gave him the notebook containing Adams's directions and descriptions as well as the map.

Dowling was an experienced miner and had worked as a commercial hunter, so he was no stranger to the outdoors and the challenges related to traveling through and surviving in the wilderness. He was also familiar with what he believed to be the mountain range in which Adams and his party had found the lost canyon of gold. In fact, Dowling had successfully panned gold from a number of small streams in the same general area.

Though not fit enough to participate in such an expedition, Dr. Spurgeon chose a close friend from Toledo to accompany Dowling and make regular reports on any progress to the physician. Dowling resented Spurgeon's assignment of a representative and told him so. Spurgeon held firm, however, and Dowling finally relented. Spurgeon's representative, as well as two other men recruited by Dowling, proved inept riders and worthless at camp chores and maintaining their stock and equipment.

Dowling claimed that during his search for the diggings, he stumbled onto a narrow cleft that opened into a zigzag canyon, which in turn led to a narrow valley through which flowed a small stream. In this valley, related Dowling, he encountered several dozen tree stumps. Given the thickness of the stumps, he reasoned that the trees had been cut down for the purpose of building a log cabin. A short distance farther up the valley, he came to a large pile of ash, charcoal, and the remains of burnt logs. At the time, Dowling was unaware of the large cache of gold nuggets lying in a hidden chamber next to a stone hearth.

Turning his attention to the stream, Dowling unpacked his pan, dipped it into the gravels, and was delighted to find some gold flake. For almost a week, Dowling panned the creek and retrieved what he claimed was a small amount of ore.

Exploring a short distance upstream, Dowling came to a waterfall that he estimated to be twelve feet high. Beyond the waterfall, he found the remains of what he believed to be an Indian campground. For reasons unknown, Dowling never panned for gold in the stream above the waterfall. He never explained why.

Though he found some gold, Dowling later said he was unimpressed with the quantity. His brief experience in the canyon, however, convinced him it was likely the one in which Adams and his party had recovered a fortune in gold nuggets. Dowling left the canyon, never to return.

Several weeks later, Dowling told Spurgeon that the canyon warranted a second look. The two men talked briefly of another expedition to the area. Around this time, however, Dowling accepted an offer of a promising mining opportunity elsewhere. Before leaving, Dowling gave the map and notes that had once belonged to Dr. Spurgeon to an acquaintance named Ellis. Ellis later told Dowling he followed the directions and found the canyon. He reported that he located the remains of a burnt cabin and found the stone hearth, but was unable to find any gold in the hearth, the creek, or anywhere else in the canyon. Years later, however, Dowling learned that Ellis had made up the story. In truth, he never visited the canyon at all. He merely rode to the ranch of a friend and remained there until it was time to return.

After working as a mine supervisor in Colorado and Wyoming for thirty years, Dowling returned to New Mexico but never undertook a return trip to the Lost Adams Diggings.

Adams continued to travel and explore throughout Arizona and New Mexico during the 1870s and early 1880s. His objectives remain unclear, and his motives have been subjected to a great deal of criticism and suspicion. Some claim he was still searching for the lost canyon of gold, and others insist he was pursuing business opportunities. Some of a more cynical nature suspected Adams of attempting to recruit investors to hire him to lead them to the lost diggings. During his travels, Adams drank heavily and was rarely seen sober.

During one of Adams's expeditions into west-central New Mexico, a man approached him and introduced himself as Bob Lewis. Lewis told Adams that he had searched for years for the lost canyon of gold but with no success. During his conversations with Adams, Lewis gleaned even more information he was determined to employ on his next expedition. Weeks later, Lewis found himself in the heart of the Datil Mountains in west-central New Mexico, where, he claimed, he finally found the lost placer mine. The Datils are located eighty straight-line miles northeast of the Mogollons, a horse ride of several days over very rough country.

Lewis claimed he had found the narrow, partially concealed entrance to the zigzag canyon. On entering, he stated, he encountered the skeletal remains of several men and a number of horses, as well as pieces of packsaddles, all stuffed into a crevice. These, he concluded, were the remains of the Brewer party Adams sent for supplies.

Lewis's claims are suspect. It is difficult to believe that the Apache Indians, who viewed horses and mules as vital to their culture and survival, would kill those animals. It is possible that one or two of the animals could have perished during the ambush, but the notion that a "number" of them were slain is difficult to believe.

Invoking some elements of Adams's tale, Lewis claimed he rode through a Z-shaped canyon, eventually coming out into a small clearing. Along the bottom of the canyon ran a narrow, shallow stream. Near the clearing, he set up camp and panned for a week in the hope of finding gold. During his stay in the canyon, Lewis's explorations took him upstream, where he said he came to a twelve-foot-high waterfall. Inexplicably, though aware of the story of Adams's party finding gold nuggets the size of a hen's egg in the stream above the falls, Lewis said he made no attempt to pan there. This, of course, creates more doubt as to the credibility of his tale.

After a week of panning, Lewis said, he had harvested just enough gold to fill half a small ore sack. Finally growing discouraged, he broke camp, left the canyon, and returned to his home in Magdalena, New Mexico.

During the summer of 1886, Adams was searching for his lost diggings in the mountains near present-day Clifton, Arizona, when he suffered a severe heart attack. He was carried out of the rugged area by members of his party, transported to the nearest railroad station, and sent home to California. There, he died on September 21.

Little did Adams know that during this trip he was geographically closer to relocating his famous lost canyon of gold than ever.

✢ 10 ✢

The Return of John Brewer

During the summer of 1888, a man accompanied by his Indian wife and small daughter pulled two freight wagons up to the ranch house of Ammon Tenny. The man drove one, and his wife and daughter drove the other. The Tenny Ranch was located near Round Valley, Arizona (now Springerville). In the most often quoted account of the visit, J. Frank Dobie has this event taking place thirty miles to the north, not far from the present-day town of St. Johns, Arizona. Dobie also misspelled Tenny's name as Tenney.

Behind the newcomers' wagons trailed a herd of twenty cattle and six horses. When Tenny came out the front door and onto the porch, the driver of the wagon climbed down, introduced himself as John Brewer, and said he had just come from Colorado. He requested permission to camp nearby and graze his tired and hungry stock for a few days. Tenny welcomed the stranger and pointed toward a suitable location a few hundred yards away, where he would find some decent graze for the animals and a clear-water stream. There were also cottonwoods and willows along the stream bank for a windbreak and firewood. Brewer thanked Tenny, climbed back onto his wagon, and hied his team toward the spot.

Later that evening, rancher Tenny rode over to the site to visit with the weary travelers and make certain they had everything they needed. Over a cup of coffee brewed in an old metal pot set over some cottonwood coals, Tenny, who was familiar with the story of the Lost Adams Diggings, which was well known throughout the region, asked his visitor if he was by chance any relation to the John Brewer who had been a member of that ill-fated party. Following a long moment of silence, the newcomer admitted he was, in fact, the same man who had led the supply party and been presumed killed by Nana's Apaches at the entrance to the canyon.

For the rest of the evening, Brewer, now sixty-three years old, related to Tenny his version of finding the canyon, reaping the rich gold from the stream, and witnessing the horrible massacre at the hands of the Apaches. According to Tenny, Brewer's sense of direction and ability to recall pertinent landmarks was not much better than Adams's. Brewer, however, was convinced that Gotch Ear had led the party of miners across the Little Colorado River, which was only a day's ride from the Tenny Ranch.

As Brewer spoke of the trials and events of that time twenty-four years earlier, he clenched his jaw and gazed dully at the horizon as if trying to hold back unpleasant memories. In the Dobie version of the account, Brewer allegedly told Tenny that Apaches had attacked the party as they arrived at the entrance to the canyon on their way back from purchasing supplies. He assumed that they had been spotted by the ubiquitous sentinels. Five of his companions were killed during the initial volley of arrows. Brewer was badly wounded, taking an arrow in the left calf. He said he was so frightened that he lost control of the panicked horse he was riding. He let go of the rope to the pack animals, held tight to the saddle horn, and gave the animal its head as it fled into the canyon. When he reached a point not far from the clearing, he saw the burning log cabin and the rampaging Indians. He gazed at the mutilated bodies of his friends lying scattered across the ground.

At that moment, Brewer presumed he was the only survivor of the massacre and was not aware that Adams and Davidson were hiding in the brush only a few yards away from where he sat on his horse.

Fearful of being spotted and pursued by the Indians, Brewer hid himself and his mount in a clump of trees and waited for some time to pass. When he was certain the last of the Indians had departed, he rode back out of the canyon and fled eastward from the mountain range and into the desert. Days later, after riding for over one hundred miles, Brewer was weak and exhausted and had no food and water. He chanced upon a hunting party of friendly Indians. After sharing what they had, the Indians led the desperate Brewer to their encampment not far from the Rio Grande. Brewer said he remained at this camp for nearly three months recovering from his ordeal. When he was well enough to travel, the Indians provided him with a better horse and some provisions and bade him good fortune as he rode away.

During the next decade, Brewer was at times tempted to return to the canyon to try to retrieve the huge cache of gold he presumed still lay in the hidden chamber next to the stone hearth. He could never bring himself to do so. He came to believe the canyon was cursed. In later years, he confessed to experiencing recurring nightmares of the massacre and his flight. He thought often of the friends he lost, the men who died for violating the Apaches' sacred canyon.

For years, Brewer was unaware that Adams had survived the Indian attack. He was likewise unaware of the growing interest in what was being referred to as the Lost Adams Diggings and the subsequent numerous expeditions that had set out in search of it. Brewer had spent his time trapping and ranching in Colorado, far from newspapers and talk of the goings-on in Arizona and New Mexico. He passed more than a decade without ever learning of the elevated status of the fabled canyon of rich placer gold.

Brewer told Tenny that he had thought Adams was killed during the Indian attack in the canyon but years later heard rumors that he had survived and was leading search parties in an attempt to relocate it. Brewer chuckled at this because, as he related to Tenny, while Adams was an honorable man, he had such a poor sense of direction that couldn't find his way out of a hotel room.

The two men visited well into the night. As Tenny rose to leave for his house, Brewer told him that there was more gold in Itsnatahey Canyon than ten kings could spend in a lifetime.

During the time that John Brewer and his family remained at the Tenny Ranch, the rancher's son, Ammon Jr., visited with him often, sometimes traveling with him into the nearby mountains to hunt for deer. During that time, Brewer related even more details of his experiences with the lost canyon of gold than he had provided the boy's father. In time, young Ammon Tenny wrote down a number of aspects of the story of the Lost Adams Diggings as related by Brewer. Years later, Ammon Tenny Jr.'s recollections found their way into print, and the story he told differs markedly from J. Frank Dobie's version.

The boy went by the name A. M. Tenny Jr. as an adult. In an article published in the March 1928 issue of *Frontier Times* magazine, he offered his version of Brewer's account of what took place in the lost canyon of gold.

According to Brewer, he was not among the party of miners from Pennsylvania and Ohio, as claimed by Dobie. Brewer, in the company of four other men, had left California to try their luck at prospecting for gold and other minerals in Arizona and New Mexico. He and his friends came upon the larger party of miners by chance.

While Dobie claimed that a bargain was made with Gotch Ear to lead the miners to the lost canyon of gold in exchange for two horses, a saddle, a rifle, some ammunition, and two fifty-dollar gold pieces, Brewer related that the Mexican agreed to guide them to the location for $1,000. Significantly, in Tenny Jr.'s account, Brewer never mentioned leading an expedition to Fort Wingate, or anywhere else, for supplies, raising the possibility that he never did—that Adams or perhaps Dobie had concocted that part of the tale.

According to Tenny Jr., while Adams and a number of miners went in search of some horses that had wandered away, Brewer remained in camp to clean up around the area and wash dishes. Three of his companions decided to venture farther upstream and try their luck panning for gold in a section of the waterway they deemed promising. Accompanied by Gotch Ear, they departed. Recall that in Dobie's account, Gotch Ear, after being paid to guide the miners to this location, rode away. In Brewer's account, he remained in the miners' camp.

As Brewer busied himself in the camp, he heard the sounds of gunfire and screams. He raced a short distance from the cabin to determine the source of the disturbance and saw his friends being massacred by the Apaches. Brewer turned and fled.

Most of Brewer's account, as related by Tenny Jr., dealt with his flight from the canyon and ultimate rescue by friendly Indians. Significantly, nowhere in Brewer's telling of his experiences in the lost canyon of gold did he mention a zigzag canyon, a waterfall, or an expedition to purchase supplies.

The differences between Dobie's and Brewer's accounts are significant and telling. Brewer's version smacks of the unvarnished rendering of an experience. He told of finding gold, harvesting it, and then fleeing as a result of the Indian menace. There were no heroics, no dramatic or mythological elements of a quest replete with obstacles and threshold guardians. Dobie's telling of the story of the lost canyon of gold, on the other hand, is full of adventure and a number of elements that appear almost too good to be true (see chapter 16).

In the end, we are left asking, What is the truth about the Lost Adams Diggings? With the passage of a century and a half following Adams's visit to the canyon, it is likely that the answer to that question will remain elusive. An elusive truth, however, is not impossible to find. In the annals of professional treasure hunting, elusive truths generally turn out to be those ignored or passed by. If it exists, any truth can be found. This in itself represents the seed for a quest.

✤ 11 ✤

The German

A close acquaintance of C. A. Shaw was a man named Doc Young. Author and folklorist J. Frank Dobie once wrote that during his lifetime, Young, a miner with considerable experience, had gathered more "facts" and information about Adams's lost canyon of gold than any man living. Young was also in possession of some insight into the German who had accompanied Adams and left with the Brewer supply party.

According to Young, he was visiting acquaintances in Los Angeles when he decided to go for a walk one morning and spend some time at a favorite park. While taking sun on a bench, Young was joined by an elderly man, and the two struck up a conversation. After a while, the talk turned to mining, and Young asked the old-timer if he had ever heard the story of a rich placer mine called the Lost Adams Diggings.

Young was surprised to learn that the old fellow not only knew a great deal about the mine but also had some knowledge of the German who was a member of the Adams party but left with his own share of the gold. The old man told Young he had located the German in Heidelberg, Germany, and traveled there to talk to him about his knowledge of the canyon and its location. The German told the old man that his name was Emil Schaeffer, and by the time he finished telling his tale, Young was convinced beyond a doubt that he had indeed accompanied Adams and his party.

Schaeffer told the old man that he had failed to strike it rich while searching for ore in the California gold fields and was traveling from the West Coast to New York City when he fell in with the group of California-bound miners led by Adams. After the group arrived at Itsnatahey Canyon, the German grew concerned about the sentinels and warned Adams repeatedly to recruit some reinforcements and post extra guards against what he considered an inevitable attack by the Apaches. Schaeffer said the Indians grew angry not so much with the miners trespassing above the waterfall to pan for gold but with the construction of the log cabin. It suggested to the Apaches, according to the German, that the white men planned to remain for an extended period and intended to bring others into the canyon in the future.

The old man told Young that the German claimed he left the canyon with $10,000 worth of gold nuggets, a fortune at the time. He returned to New York, where he remained for several weeks while awaiting passage to Europe. When he finally returned to Germany, he married and raised a family.

The German provided the old man with some general directions to the canyon from Gila Bend, but like those provided by Adams, Jack Davidson, and John Brewer, they ultimately proved worthless. It had been a long time since Schaeffer had traveled to the canyon, and his memory was not keen.

Oddly, there exists a second version of what happened to the German after he left the canyon. An unverified account relates that Schaeffer traveled to Phoenix, Arizona, where he cashed in his gold and purchased a cattle ranch near Prescott. According to this version of the tale, the German died on his ranch in 1877. How he met his end was not known.

What is the truth regarding the German? For the first version, there exists only Dobie's retelling of Young's rather serendipitous meeting in a Los Angeles park with an old man who claimed to be acquainted with the German. Attempts to confirm the second version have yielded no verifiable information whatsoever. Like most aspects of the Lost Adams Diggings, this one remains shrouded in mystery.

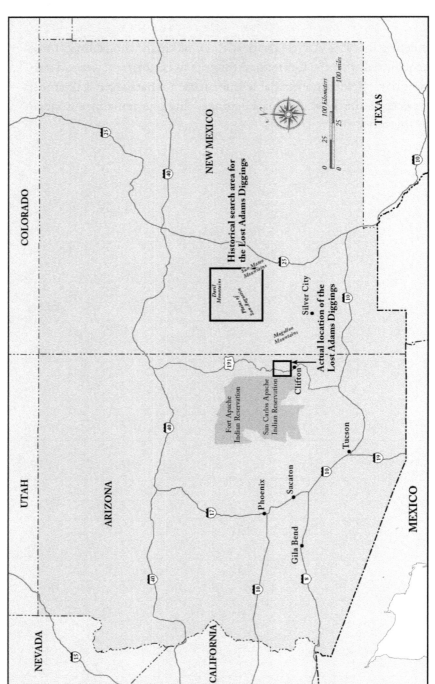

Map of the area.

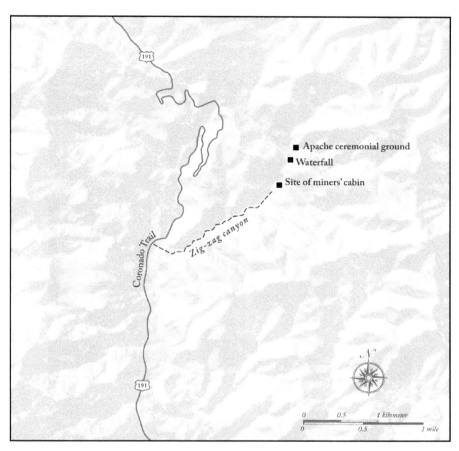

Detailed map showing the area where the Lost Adams Diggings was discovered.

Stream from which the Adams party mined gold nuggets.

Jim Peterson, who led the author to the Lost Adams Diggings.

Twin piloncillos, sugar cone-shaped mountains near the lost canyon.

One of the ridges from which Apaches observed the Adams mining party.

Abandoned line shack at the site of the Adams cabin—this more recent cabin was built around the original rock hearth, which contained secret compartments for hiding gold.

Secret compartment at the rear of the hearth.

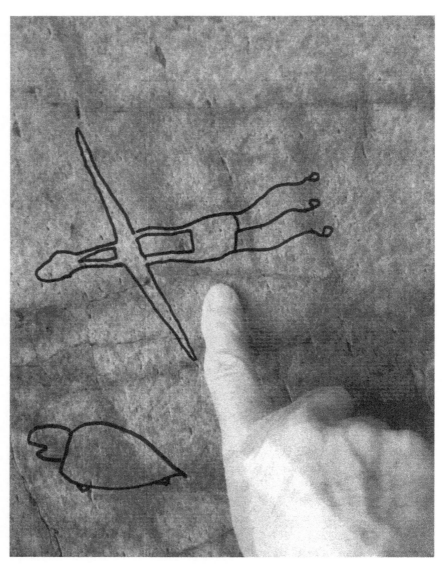

Shaman and turtle petroglyphs.

Gold nuggets in upper right of pan. *Photo by Earl Theiss.*

The author panning gold from the Adams Diggings stream. *Photo by Earl Theiss.*

Twelve-foot-high waterfall in the Lost Canyon of Gold. *Photo by Earl Theiss.*

Earl Theiss panning gold in a Lost Canyon pothole.

12

Jason Baxter's Search for the Lost Canyon of Gold

In 1877, a man named James McKenna arrived in the Black Range region of southwestern New Mexico. He spent most of his time in the area working as a miner and cowhand and during his stay came to know many of the colorful individuals who populated the area. In 1936, he published *Black Range Tales* about his experiences and adventures. In one of the chapters, McKenna relates a number of stories originally told by a man named Jason Baxter, who identified himself as a former pony express rider, scout, trapper, Indian fighter, prospector, and miner. That's a lot of adventures for one man, and the truth of his statements has never been proven. Baxter, like several other men during this time, also claimed to have found the Lost Adams Diggings.

Baxter told McKenna that he first met Adams in Arizona and later encountered him in Pinos Altos, New Mexico. Baxter was certain Adams was crazy but was also convinced that the man had, in fact, located the now famous canyon of gold that bore his name. Baxter said Adams set out in search of his lost diggings several times from Silver City, New Mexico. Each time, according to Baxter, he got lost in an area called Cactus Flats and was forced to return.

Baxter asserted that Adams's lost diggings were the same as what came to be known in the region at the time as the Lost Nigger Diggings. He related a tale about a black cavalry trooper who, while on assignment, rode into a narrow canyon, whose description fit with that of Adams's location. Here, the trooper allegedly found nuggets in abundance in a little stream that wound its way along the canyon floor. He later said the canyon was near what he identified as Island Mountain and not far from "the mountain with the painted face of a woman on the eastern side."

When discharged from the army several months later, the cavalryman returned to the canyon to harvest more of the placer gold. He had been there only a few hours and panned a significant amount of gold when several Apaches approached and chased him away. Fearing for his life, the cavalryman, as far as anyone knew, never returned to the canyon.

Baxter insisted this same location was also referred to as the Snively Diggings, which predated Adams's visit to the area. According to Baxter, a man named Snively had reportedly found a rich placer mine in a remote canyon, whose description was also similar to that of the one found by Adams. From the little stream that ran through the canyon, Snively panned approximately $10,000 worth of gold before abandoning the location and traveling to Fort West. Snively, it was said, was a reliable and trustworthy man and a founder of the New Mexico town of Pinos Altos. Baxter claimed Snively told him that a few Mexican sheepherders also knew about the canyon and the gold it contained but, fearing the Apaches, never attempted to retrieve any of the ore. Baxter also stated that, in addition to being known as the Snively Diggings, the Adams Diggings, and the Lost Nigger Diggings, the location was also called the Schaeffer Diggings. It is unclear why Baxter believed this. To further complicate matters, around this time prospectors and miners were referring to a number of other placer gold discoveries in widely varying locations throughout New Mexico and Arizona as the Lost Adams Diggings.

Baxter claimed he learned the story of the Schaeffer Diggings from a man named McGurk. While a sergeant in the army, McGurk was placed in charge of a team of woodcutters. The woodsmen, accompanied by a platoon of armed troopers, left Fort Cummings, located about fifteen miles northeast of Deming, New Mexico, and traveled to the headwaters of the Mimbres River to procure wood for the fort. This was a dangerous area, for Apache chief Victorio was thought to maintain a stronghold nearby. A cook named Jacob Schaeffer, apparently no relation to the German Emil Schaeffer, accompanied the woodcutters. His job was to keep the workers and the soldiers fed, as well as to procure game for the pot.

One day, after they had been in the area cutting wood for three months, McGurk sent Schaeffer out to hunt for game, preferably deer, for the stewpot. It was a risk, McGurk acknowledged, for Schaeffer had a notoriously poor sense of direction and was always getting lost, even within a few dozen yards of the camp. His hunting excursions often necessitated the organization and deployment of a search party.

When Schaeffer did not return in a reasonable time, McGurk and another soldier set out on horseback looking for him. They found Schaeffer's tracks and encountered the carcass of a deer he had shot, but they could not locate the cook. As they looked for Schaeffer, Apaches attacked. Abandoning the search, the two soldiers returned to the camp as fast as their horses could carry them. On arriving, they found that the site had been raided by Indians. Several woodcutters and two troopers were dead. McGurk ordered the rest of the men to pack only necessary items, and they quickly fled the area. They presumed Schaeffer had met his fate at the hands of the Apaches.

A few days later, McGurk, accompanied by twenty mounted and armed troopers from Fort Cummings, returned to the site to bury the dead men. Following this, they went in search of the Indians in the hope of encountering them and driving them from the region. They followed the tracks of the Apaches for several miles toward the north but were unable to overtake them. The troopers returned to the fort.

When McGurk and the soldiers arrived back at Fort Cummings, they learned that Schaeffer had been found. After wandering for days lost in the mountains, he walked into Fort Craig 30 miles south of Socorro and approximately 120 miles northeast of the woodcutters' campsite. Those who saw Schaeffer when he arrived said he was barefoot, nearly naked, weaponless, and acting "crazy as a loon," according to Baxter. He also toted a haversack that contained ten pounds of large nuggets of pure gold.

Days later, when he had recovered, Schaeffer told of his experiences as best he could remember them. He said he was hunting for deer when he spotted a big buck forty yards away in the woods. His shot struck the deer, but the animal bounded away deeper into the trees. Schaeffer went in search of it but became lost. He had no idea where he was and no clue how to get back to the camp. He picked a direction and started walking. He never saw the Apaches who attacked McGurk. He said he crossed a wide plain that contained a lot of wild horses and herds of antelope. According to McGurk, the description matched only the Plains of San Augustin, eighty miles north of where Schaeffer originally became lost. An extensive flat expanse south of the Datil Mountains, the plains cover in excess of six hundred square miles and are hard to ignore or overlook. They were never mentioned by Adams, Davidson, or Brewer.

Schaeffer, like the black cavalryman before him, claimed he spotted a mountain "with a woman's picture painted on it in bright colors." Sometime and somewhere after that he stumbled into a narrow canyon, where he found a small stream filled with gold nuggets.

Based on Schaeffer's descriptions, McGurk narrowed down the location of the mysterious canyon to somewhere between the headwaters of New Mexico's Mimbres River and Arizona's Little Colorado River, a rather wide swath of land considering that the two rivers are approximately 120 miles apart. However, a branch of Carrizo Wash, a tributary of the Little Colorado River, originates on the western slope of the Datil Mountains, the range mentioned earlier by Bob Lewis.

The veracity of Schaeffer's account, or perhaps McGurk's interpretation of it, warrants a closer look. If Schaeffer had indeed ventured into or near the Plains of San Augustin, he could have done so only after trekking northward across a rugged set of mountains. Once there, he had to have made a ninety-degree turn to the east to arrive at Fort Craig. Any analyst would consider this a rather bizarre route, even for someone who was allegedly directionally impaired.

McGurk said he knew of the mountain with the image of a woman on it and believed its actual name was Mount Magdalena. He said that on the east side of this mountain, shadows cast by natural rock outcrops and formations resembled the head and face of a woman and were easily discerned. McGurk said he believed the Spanish called the mountain Our Lady of Magdalena and that it was located at the north end of the Black Range near the edge of the Plains of San Augustin. To the east was Fort Craig.

When finally discharged from the army, McGurk decided to go in search of the Schaeffer Diggings. First, however, he planned to visit relatives in his hometown of Columbus, Ohio. He spent two months there, ran out of money, and reenlisted in the army. He never returned to New Mexico to search for the gold.

Baxter was somehow convinced that the gold associated with Snively, Adams, the black cavalryman, and Schaeffer all came from the same place. Furthermore, Baxter claimed that he had located the canyon himself and was now calling the placer gold deposit he found there the Baxter Diggings.

Baxter maintained these diggings were located north and east of Fort West. He said Snively had traveled south from his alleged canyon of gold for 125 miles before arriving at the fort. He also said Snively had spoken of Indian sentinels watching him from the ridge tops and that they had frightened him out of the canyon. Once he had escaped with his life and saddlebags filled with gold nuggets, Snively never had any desire to go back.

Baxter entered the Datil range and set a course for a peak he called Island Mountain. (According to some old-timers in the area, this mountain today is known as Volcanic Hub.) One night while camping, according to Baxter, one of his mules broke the picket rope and wandered away toward the east. The next morning, Baxter followed it, tracking it through canyons and across low ridges. At one point, he found himself atop a ridge from which he claimed he could see the White Mountains of Arizona to the northwest. Baxter also said he could see the mule about half a mile ahead of him.

Baxter, following the mule, rode to one end of the ridge, dropped down into a wooded canyon, and came to what appeared to be a sheer wall. The mule, however, kept going and passed through a narrow opening in the rock. Baxter trailed the animal and found himself making his way through the entrance and following a canyon through which flowed a small stream. As he rode through the canyon, Baxter saw numerous signs of Indians.

Baxter finally caught up with the mule late in the afternoon and decided to camp in the canyon for the night. Nervous about all the Indian signs he had seen on the way in, he constructed a low breastwork of rocks, placing a portion of the canyon wall with a slight overhang at his back. As he worked, growing storm clouds, accompanied by thunder and lightning, passed over the canyon.

It was dark by the time Baxter had finished his dinner and was sipping coffee beneath the rock overhang. The storm increased in intensity and rain fell harder, but his shelter offered some modicum of protection.

Just as Baxter was growing drowsy from the day's activities and looked forward to a good night's sleep, the Apaches attacked.

Dozens of arrows flew into and over his breastwork, some landing dangerously close to him. He decided he could not survive a continued attack and believed his only chance was to make a run for it. Jumping onto his horse and grabbing the lead rope of the mule, Baxter fled the canyon. The Apaches, on foot, were close behind. During his flight, Baxter related, flashes of lightning illuminated portions of the landscape through which he rode, helping him find his way. During one bright flash, Baxter said he saw a burnt-down log cabin with "no roof and only a few logs standing." Scattered across the ground near the cabin were bleached white bones. Later, Baxter told someone he thought the bones belonged to men and not animals. Nearby, next to the stream, he said, he spotted an old sluice box used to mine placer gold.

Baxter escaped the canyon well ahead of the Apaches and spurred his horse toward the west. He climbed a ridge, looked to the south, and spotted what he believed were the San Mateo Mountains. At this point, Baxter said he traveled southward, heading for the northern end of the Mogollon Mountains. There, he claimed, he struck the headwaters of what he identified as the "Frisco River" just west of Clifton.

When Baxter finally returned to civilization, he declared to all who would listen that Adams's lost canyon of gold was near Island Mountain in the Datil range. Many who listened to his tale accepted it at face value and credited him with finally locating the Lost Adams Diggings. Baxter's oft-told version appears to have settled in as the definitive one regarding a specific location of the diggings.

Months passed, and Baxter decided to undertake another expedition into the Datil Mountains to the lost canyon of gold. Alone, he undertook a different route this time but still arrived at the western end of the range. Riding into what he was convinced was the correct canyon, he became confused. From where he camped that night, he insisted, he could see the woman's face on Mount Magdalena to the southwest.

With some difficulty, Baxter found the route he followed when he was tracking the mule that had broken away from his camp during his earlier visit. He arrived at Island Mountain, looked around, and found everything changed. He said it appeared as though a great earthquake had occurred since his last visit, rearranging everything such that it was unrecognizable and filling the canyon with tons of rock debris. Nothing, he said, looked the same. Despite Baxter's observation, however, no "great earthquake" had been recorded in the region during this or any other time. The Lost Adams Diggings, according to Jason Baxter, were buried beneath several feet of rock.

Baxter could not have been more mistaken.

⁙ 13 ⁙

Sentinels

During the 1930s, noted author and folklorist J. Frank Dobie, in compiling information about the Lost Adams Diggings, was given the name of a man who had been chief of scouts on an Apache Indian reservation during the 1880s. The man, according to what he told Dobie, had also worked as a cowhand for a number of ranches, purchased weapons and ammunition for warring Yaqui Indians in Mexico, rode with Teddy Roosevelt's Rough Riders, tracked the Apache Kid, soldiered in the French army, and mined gold in Mexico. The man's name was James B. Gray, and he told Dobie that he knew the precise location of the lost canyon of gold.

According to Gray, Adams provided numerous accounts of his initial journey from Gila Bend to the fabled lost diggings, every one of them different. He also reiterated that Adams had a bad memory and was unskilled at traveling in the wilderness. Gray also substantiated the notion that, in his later years, Adams drank heavily and had difficulty remembering anything. It is not clear how Gray came to meet Adams. It is also important to note that, alcohol use aside, it had already been substantiated time and again that Adams couldn't remember much of anything even when he was sober.

Gray insisted the two major rivers crossed by the Adams party were not the Little Colorado and the Black, which would have the party traveling in a definite northeasterly direction, but rather the

San Pedro and the Gila, which would have them moving generally eastward. A short time after crossing the last big river, the band of miners entered the small mountain range that contained the mysterious canyon. Gray maintained that it was located not far from, and east of, the San Carlos Apache Indian Reservation in southeastern Arizona.

According to Dobie, Gray knew Indians and was particularly knowledgeable about the Apaches. He related that Chief Nana's Apache sentinels kept the Adams party under surveillance from the moment they entered the mountain range. Gray also stated that when he was chief of scouts on the San Carlos reservation, he was always conscious of being watched by Indian sentinels whenever he entered the mountains to the east, particularly in the area of a certain canyon known to be sacred to the Apaches.

One day, Gray decided to ride to this canyon and conduct a surreptitious exploration and search for Adams's famous gold placer. He guided his horse through the narrow entrance and followed a zigzag trail until it opened into a small clearing. All the while, Gray was aware of being observed by Indians stationed along the ridge tops.

During the exploration of the canyon, Gray came upon an old, burnt-out cabin that matched the descriptions provided by Adams and Brewer. As he inspected the remains of the cabin, he was conscious of being watched. Then, he said, he found the rich placer.

At one point, Gray dismounted next to a shallow creek not far from the cabin site. He pretended to check out the left front hoof of his horse. While he did so, he reached into the creek and pretended he was searching for a rock with which to hammer an ostensibly loose horseshoe. As he poked around in the shallow water, Gray managed to withdraw four large gold nuggets. After pocketing them, he remounted his horse and rode away.

Excited by his discovery, Gray returned to the same location several weeks later. Despite the nagging feeling that he was being watched, Gray searched the shallow stream and withdrew several more nuggets. As he was examining his newfound wealth, he heard the sound of hoof beats. He turned and saw a dozen mounted Apaches riding toward him from the upstream direction. Convinced the Indians were hostile, Gray jumped upon his horse and fled. One month later he sold the nuggets for sixty-two dollars.

A year after finding the gold in the canyon, Gray returned. He set up a small camp next to the stream and made plans to spend several days panning for more of the precious metal. On the second morning, as he was kneeling on the stream bank and swirling gravels around in the pan, he found himself surrounded by eight armed Apaches. He never heard them approach.

The Indians tied Gray to a tree, appearing intent on torturing and killing him, when a weathered Apache elder arrived and ordered him set free. The Indian, said Gray, was a medicine man named Go-sho-nay. He and Gray had been close friends at the San Carlos reservation and often took their evening meals together. The old Apache told Gray he would be released if he vowed never to return to the canyon. If the promise were broken, he warned, Gray would be killed. Gray was only too happy to agree. Go-sho-nay told Gray that the canyon, called Itsnatahey, was sacred to the Apaches and always under watch, day and night, in all seasons.

The story of Indian sentinels watching over the lost canyon of gold has been related many times by men convinced they have found Adams's lost diggings. It was a story heard by miners, prospectors, and other seekers of the famous lost placer mine. It was a story told by hikers and riders who chanced into the region, men who knew nothing of the gold to be found there. It was an observation made by men who were part of the road gang that constructed a major north-south route that passed near the mouth of the canyon.

Today, there is some evidence that Indian sentinels continue to watch over the canyon. Some say they are armed and may have killed men who desecrated this sacred location. Such stories have never been substantiated.

PART III

Analysis

✢ 14 ✢

A Survey of the Literature

One thing that seems to have escaped the notice of most people who have indulged in a study of or search for the Lost Adams Diggings is that any serious and competently conducted research and investigation into a topic is always preceded by a survey of the pertinent extant literature. Far too often, writers and self-proclaimed treasure hunters undertake a project after reading only one or two articles or book chapters on a subject. Unfortunately, such a cursory and limited examination of the available information provides the seeker with a paucity of knowledge that, as experience has shown time and again, normally leads to negative and misleading results as well as to a significant waste of time and energy.

There is precious little factual and competently researched and written literature related to the Lost Adams Diggings. A selected bibliography of what has been available over the years is offered at the end of this text.

The most popular book associated with the Lost Adams Diggings is *Apache Gold and Yaqui Silver*, an eminently readable tome penned by the great Texas folklorist and author J. Frank Dobie and published in 1928 by Bramhall House of New York. The book was illustrated with remarkable pen and ink renderings by the famous El Paso, Texas, artist Tom Lea. It has been reprinted numerous times.

Apache Gold and Yaqui Silver is an important book because it introduced thousands to some of the most amazing tales and legends of lost mines and buried treasures associated with the southwestern United States and Mexico. Indeed, many a hopeful treasure hunter set out on his quest to locate the Lost Adams Diggings after reading this publication.

Dobie was an adept storyteller. He traveled the United States and Mexico in search of stories, interviewing men with knowledge and experience related to topics he was interested in. While grateful to Dobie for his research and his writings, as well as his inspiration, I am forced to admit that Dobie devoted more attention to the actual telling of the story than he did to the truth. It is not that Dobie ever deliberately falsified anything; he simply never let the truth get in the way of a good tale. He claimed, on at least one occasion, that it was his job as a storyteller to relate the tale as best he could, often improving it along the way. No stranger to mythology, Dobie wove elements of some of the world's most popular myths into his own writings. Thus, when applying Dobie's work to any search for the Lost Adams Diggings, one must separate the myth from the truth.

Another source of the Lost Adams Diggings legend, one that predates Dobie's book and from which Dobie gleaned a critical amount of information, was a self-published pamphlet by W. H. Byerts titled *Gold: The Adams Gold Diggings*, released in 1919. Byerts learned the story of the Lost Adams Diggings from C. A. Shaw, so most of his information was second-hand, and some of it was even third- and fourth-hand. Byerts sold only a handful of his pamphlets before he passed away a few years after the document's publication.

While many students of the Adams diggings regard Byerts's pamphlet as a source of important knowledge, it is filled with misinformation and many so-called facts that were inferred rather than substantiated. In one passage Byerts writes, "According to Adams, the course they took from the Pima villages . . . would land the [canyon] in the northern part of [New Mexico's] Socorro County . . . as the point of the Malpais mountains is in Socorro County."

In the first place, such information was not "according to Adams." It was, in fact, according to Shaw, who related to Byerts what he thought he remembered Adams saying. In the second place, as the following pages will show, it would have been impossible for Adams and his party to reach this location, or anyplace near it, in the stated time of travel. In the third place, there are no "Malpais mountains" in Socorro County. *Malpais* is a Spanish word (literal translation: "badlands" or "evil country") that refers to extensive lava flows, some of which can be found in the once volcanically active region of west-central New Mexico; few, if any, can be found in Socorro County.

I refer here to Byerts's mention of "the point of the Malpais mountains" because a handful of subsequent researchers and writers placed far more faith in that alleged directional statement than was ever warranted. There does exist, however, a Malpais Mountain associated with the Lost Adams Diggings, but it is located at least 140 straight-line miles southwest of the Socorro County location.

Another book from which Dobie pulled information on the diggings was *Black Range Tales*, a fascinating collection by a man named James A. McKenna and originally published by Wilson-Erickson, Inc., of New York in 1936. Like Dobie's *Apache Gold and Yaqui Silver*, it is a compelling book containing a collection of yarns gathered over a number of years. The book is exciting, entertaining, and eminently readable. Unfortunately, while McKenna weaves a fine story, little of the publication possesses much veracity.

In 1935, noted treasure writer John D. Mitchell released *Lost Mines of the Great Southwest*, published by the Journal Company, Inc., in Phoenix, Arizona. For many years, Mitchell's book was a principal reference for anyone interested in lost mines and buried treasures located in this geographical region. Many still refer to it. For those interested in solid, pertinent information and fact, however, this book does not offer much. Mitchell's writing style is easy and comfortable, but he was primarily a collector of tales and simply retold them in his own style. As far as I can determine, he had little to no first-hand knowledge of or experience with any of them and conducted no significant research beyond locating and acquiring good stories, many of which contained errors and misinformation.

A more recent book is *Four Days from Fort Wingate: The Lost Adams Diggings* by Richard French (published by the Caxton Printers, Ltd., 1994). I have read and reread this book a number of times in attempts to glean some sense of it, but it eludes me. The author was so seduced by the myth of the Adams treasure that it appears to have clouded his reasoning. The book manifests little or no fact-checking, logic, or even editing.

French's search for the Lost Adams Diggings appears to have been more hobby than professional quest. The odd journalistic style (which includes fake names for himself and his wife), the disjointed organization, and the strange interpretations of history and geography render this publication somewhat confusing and contradictory. The book is replete with misinterpretations of land-scapes, distances, and logistics. French, in fact, appears obsessed to distraction with Byerts's reference to the "point of the Malpais." So much hinges on this alleged and unlikely geographic landmark in the French book as to cause the reader to wonder what he was thinking and why he wasted so much ink on this particular land-scape feature.

A handful of other books have been penned on the subject of the Lost Adams Diggings. All of them cling in one way or another to the prevailing story originally interpreted by Dobie and his sources and offer nothing new. All those I have encountered do little more than repeat old information and contain nothing in the way of original research or pertinent insight. Most were self-published and manifest the characteristics associated with such work: poor or no editing, amateurish design and format-ting, and, worst of all, no investigation, deconstruction, analysis, reconstruction, and fact-checking. These publications serve no purpose whatsoever except to perpetuate the original, and often misleading, tales associated with the famous diggings.

The majority of the available literature associated with the Lost Adams Diggings is in the form of newspaper and magazine articles. In the latter part of the nineteenth century, the story of the diggings was on the lips of those oriented toward such compelling tales of lost mines and buried treasure. Since the public has long craved such tales of finding and losing wealth, the tellers found eager publishing outlets in periodicals. Newspapers in the American Southwest were particularly prone to publish such pieces. Early on, magazines such as *Frontier Times*, *Adventure*, *New Mexico*, and others couldn't get enough of these tales. Since the 1960s, a spate of treasure-oriented magazines have become players in the field of publishing articles about treasure hunting, prospecting, and metal detecting. Thanks to page after page advertising metal detectors and prospecting gear, these magazines managed to survive for a while. Today there are fewer of them, but those that remain appear healthy and adequately serve the interests of subscribers. One can count on them to publish something about the Lost Adams Diggings every so often. Alas, as with the books, none of the articles offer new or helpful information. They are rarely, if ever, subjected to fact-checking or editing and invariably provide examples of more repetition accompanied by no original research or personal experience.

I have noticed that a few of the more recent articles related to the Lost Adams Diggings pertain to a so-called discovery of the canyon and an announcement that the author has "found" the fabled lost placer mine. On reading the articles, however, one finds that the claim of discovery is based on spurious evidence. Someone will have hiked into a zigzag canyon and come away convinced that it is the one associated with Adams's original expedition. Someone else will discover a rock hearth remaining in an old cabin site and jump to the conclusion that it is the one constructed by Adams and his party.

None of these articles pull together all the important eviden-tial elements. A hearth or a zigzag canyon by itself is not evidence of the lost canyon of gold. To make a serious claim of discovery, one has to have, within the confines of the canyon, evidence con-sisting of a "secret door," a pumpkin patch, a zigzag canyon, a rock hearth containing a secret chamber, a twelve-foot-tall waterfall, an Apache campsite/ceremonial ground, two sugar-cone-shaped peaks nearby, and, most importantly, a stream containing placer gold. The truth is, none of these prior claims hold up because little of the crucial evidence is apparent.

Direction, Distance, Geography, and Logic

During the past century and a half people have been searching for, as well as claiming discovery of, Adams's lost canyon of gold. However, a number of significant logistical considerations, geographic obstacles, and other problems throw their alleged discoveries into doubt:

1. None of the searchers knew the precise direction in which the canyon lay from Adams's initial point of origin, Gila Bend.

2. No one had any accurate insight into the geographic distance between Gila Bend and the canyon of gold.

3. The exact amount of time it took for the party of miners to travel from the point of origin to the destination has never been substantiated. Estimates provided by Adams ranged from eight to fourteen days, and none of those can be trusted.

4. No one knew the correct name of the mountain range in which the canyon of gold was located.

5. No one knew for certain which mountains and mountain ranges lay between the point of origin and the canyon of gold. These would amount to significant landscape features to be traversed during the journey.

6. No one knew the exact rivers, major and minor, crossed during the initial trip to the canyon.
7. All the so-called discoveries of the Lost Adams Diggings made by a variety of men have been in different locations, some of which were more than one hundred miles apart.

Through the years, dozens, perhaps hundreds, of men searching for the lost diggings would show up in towns and villages throughout Arizona and New Mexico claiming to have found the canyon and the rich placer stream. Others would assert that they possessed specific insight or information relative to the location. These many claims of discovery cited locations spread out over an area as large as ten thousand square miles. Clearly, all could not have been the Lost Adams Diggings. To further complicate matters, some who have felt compelled to write about the Lost Adams Diggings have made the consistent mistake of simply repeating the oft-told and scribed tales without ever doing any fact-checking or original research and investigation. As I will point out in detail, none of the writers appeared to possess any sense of geography, distance, or direction. For that matter, none of them took the time to investigate the discrepancies in all the accounts. It would be appropriate, therefore, to examine evidence that can help determine where the Lost Adams Diggings are *not* located.

The significant problems associated with distance, direction, and geography all started with Adams. From the beginning, he manifested an obvious ineptness relative to traveling in the wilderness. This lack of competence was apparent and consistent throughout all his subsequent expeditions into the area.

Adams also possessed extremely poor powers of observation and recollection. For example, when Adams once stated that he departed Tucson after dropping off a load of freight and picking up another, he claimed he passed through the Pima village called Sacaton. The truth is, Sacaton was not on the way from Tucson to

Gila Bend. In fact, it lay a considerable distance off the main road of travel, approximately twenty miles. It is absurd to believe Adams would have made such an unnecessary detour in a freight wagon while working to maintain control over a herd of twelve horses.

Adams also stated that, after passing the Pima village, he traveled another full day before setting up camp for the night at Gila Bend. Gila Bend is located just over seventy-five miles from Sacaton. Adams could not have covered this distance during that specified time in a heavily loaded wagon capable of covering no more than ten to twenty miles per day. At this point, Adams is already exhibiting significant distance and chronological inconsistencies. Any geographical information he provided after this would immediately be suspect.

On another occasion, Adams stated that after his wagon and trailer were burned, he returned to the Pima village after leaving his campsite, arriving the same day. Clearly, Adams was confused and not to be trusted with information relating to distance and time. It is impossible that he could have arrived at Sacaton that soon after leaving his camp. More likely he encountered a small Pima encampment located one day's travel to the east of Gila Bend and not the main village seventy-five miles away.

The evidence also reveals that Adams erroneously identified mountain peaks and ranges that he passed, as well as rivers that he crossed. It will be remembered that Adams named and pointed out these features and landforms in a portion of Arizona that he had never previously visited. Why Adams made any attempt to identify and provide names for features and forms of which he was completely ignorant adds another layer of confusion to an already disoriented journey.

The original trip from Gila Bend to the lost canyon of gold was, according to the descriptions, long and tiring. Some have suggested that monotony may have played a role in Adams's ignoring or disregarding important landmarks such as mountain peaks and major rivers. More likely, Adams was simply unskilled at geographic observation. During the initial trip, Adams and the rest of the party of miners relied upon their guide, Gotch Ear, and apparently paid scant attention to their surroundings. When Adams did comment on a particular mountain, range, or river, he was often wrong in his identification. In the end, Adams recognized not a single one of the pertinent landmarks during more than a dozen subsequent expeditions organized to find the lost canyon.

Adams may have relied on identifications made by others who had no more experience than he. During his return trips throughout the area, Adams may have employed maps bearing the names of the landforms and simply chosen them.

Adams claimed to have crossed two major rivers, the Black and the Little Colorado. If true, this would have placed the party in the Holbrook–St. Johns area of east-central Arizona. Another time, Adams stated the party had crossed the San Francisco River. Adams may have crossed the Little Colorado River or the San Francisco River but not both unless he traveled a considerable distance out of the way. The San Francisco River is one hundred miles south-southeast of the Little Colorado, and crossing both would have necessitated traveling for days in a different direction.

Adams also relied on and related certain information he obtained from Gotch Ear, such as the identification of the wagon road they crossed, which supposedly led to Fort Wingate. According to Adams, this event occurred just after they crossed the Little Colorado River. At this point—and the party was still in Arizona—Fort Wingate would have been located one hundred straight-line miles to the northeast, not to the north. Who is to say that Gotch Ear's information was accurate? To compound this problem, research has revealed that a major road leading south from Fort Wingate did not exist during that time. So the Fort Wingate reference point must be discarded.

Adams's sometime partner C. A. Shaw was convinced that the supply party led by John Brewer did not travel to Fort Wingate at all but rather to Fort West, located near Silver City, 120 straight-line miles south of Fort Wingate.

Adams originally stated that the party of miners led by Gotch Ear traveled by horseback for fourteen days. Years later, he said the journey took only eight days. This is a huge difference, and it is inconceivable that a person, even Adams, would confuse fourteen days with eight.

A closer examination of the geography of the region in question, along with the mode of travel, is warranted. It is extraordinary that, given the acute interest in the Lost Adams Diggings over the past 150 years, this has not been undertaken before now.

Adams and his party departed Gila Bend with a total of twenty-six horses, six of which were the draft animals that had pulled the freighter's wagon and trailer. Some of the miners rode horses, and we can assume that several of them walked, as a few of the animals were likely used to transport supplies and equipment. According to professional packers, it is rare for a pack train to cover more than twenty miles per day. This distance is within the realm of possibility when traveling under the best of conditions on level ground, but the Adams party traversed rugged mountain ranges and forded rivers while crossing the uneven, roadless terrain of eastern Arizona. Adams's stout draft horses, though undoubtedly strong and steady performers, would have not been much for speed or travel over rough, mountainous landscapes.

If we assume that Adams's party managed to complete an average of fifteen miles per day, a generous estimate given the difficult country, and traveled in a straight line, which the men assuredly did not, then at the end of the fourteenth day, assuming they had headed northeastward, they would only have arrived in the area of the Little Colorado River near St. Johns. This location is a long way from the Datil Mountains, the long-accepted and consensual location of the Lost Adams Diggings for many. At this point, the Datil Mountains still lay more than one hundred miles away to the east, requiring a minimum of another week of travel, assuming a straight, flat road with no obstacles. On the other hand, if the party were following a more eastward course, the end of the fourteenth day would have found them in the area of the San Francisco River near the Arizona–New Mexico border and not far from the present-day town of Clifton, Arizona.

Assuming for a moment the far-fetched possibility that the Lost Adams Diggings existed in the Datil Mountains in New Mexico, we must take into account that this range is located some three hundred straight-line miles from Gila Bend. Traveling at fifteen miles per day, the trip would take at least twenty days following a direct route on good roads over flat terrain. Considering the number of significant mountain ranges and major rivers they must cross during the journey, as well as the winding roads and trails, if any existed at all, it is inconceivable that this group could have made it in fourteen days. Under real-life conditions, they would need possibly a month and a half or more, a conservative estimate. Thus, given an infusion of reason, logic, mathematical calculation, and intense scrutiny of the original story and its descendants, the Datil Mountains of west-central New Mexico must be discarded as a realistic location for the Lost Adams Diggings.

In retracing Adams's route based on his descriptions as interpreted by J. Frank Dobie in *Apache Gold and Yaqui Silver*, one encounters numerous contradictions. It is not known, and likely never will be, whether Dobie accurately related Adams's directions and descriptions of the geography. Dobie, as pointed out earlier, often enriched his tales above and beyond the truth.

It is also worth pointing out that Dobie learned the distances, directions, and locations associated with Adams's lost canyon of gold second-hand, and in some cases third- and fourth-hand. In his later years, Dobie admitted to often embellishing the stories he wrote, stating that many didn't happen exactly as he had depicted and that he chose to relate, as he said, what should have happened. Dobie was noted for taking a simple tale and making it more elaborate and exciting that it really was.

Dobie also wrote that the party of miners entered the mysterious canyon and rode down into it as they followed a stream. In truth, however, the stream was flowing out of the canyon; the party entered the canyon and rode up into it. The principle of gravity dictates that water always flows downhill. Dobie made a mistake and few caught it. It must be remembered that there was a water-fall located a short distance upstream from the place where they panned most of the gold and constructed the cabin. Perhaps Dobie had no more of a sense of distance, direction, and geography, or gravity, for that matter, than did Adams.

When Adams and Davidson fled the canyon following the Indian attack, Adams stated that they rode away toward the west and were found days later by a contingent of cavalry and transported to Fort Apache. Straight-line, flat distance from the Datil Mountains to Fort Apache is approximately 120 miles. The charitable average of fifteen miles per day for travel means that the two men had to have ridden for a minimum of eight days before encountering the soldiers who rescued them. If the diggings had been located in the Datil Mountains as many insist, then Adams and Davidson would have had to cross several mountain ranges, including the Gallos, the Mogollons, and the San Franciscos, to end up where the US Army found them. This would have cut their miles per day of travel dramatically. Importantly, neither Adams nor Davidson ever mentioned crossing a single range.

Another significant problem in locating the lost diggings had to do with the distance from the canyon to Fort Wingate. Adams said he allowed eight days for the Brewer supply party to travel from the diggings to the military post and return. How he arrived at this calculation we cannot know. Adams found the remains of the massacred party on the ninth day at the entrance of the can-yon. The Datil Mountains are ninety straight-line miles southeast of Fort Wingate. Thus, using the same logic already incorporated into estimating travel on horseback in this kind of terrain, it would have taken the miners a minimum of six days to travel from the canyon to the fort, and this is being very conservative. Thus, it would take an absolute minimum of twelve days to make the complete round trip, and that's not including any significant time to round up supplies once they arrived at the fort.

Given this, the time frame of eight days for the round trip to Fort Wingate is not only unrealistic but impossible. On the other hand, if one places the prospective location for the canyon of gold near Clifton, Arizona, then Fort Apache would have been considerably closer at only four days' travel to the northwest. Fort Thomas, due west, was even nearer and would have been a more efficient trip, assuming anyone in the party knew of its existence.

Could Adams have been mistaken when he claimed the supply party traveled to Fort Wingate? It would seem likely, since Adams's recollection of everything else related to the trip was erroneous or convoluted, and his estimates of distance, direction, and geography cannot be trusted. Furthermore, there is enough mistaken and/or confusing detail in the account attributed to him to cause even the most gullible and inexperienced researcher to question its veracity.

The only logical conclusion is that the Adams party did not travel as far as the Datil Mountains or anywhere near them. Therefore, it is completely out of the realm of possibility that the lost diggings would be found in that range. The truth is, the Adams party never made it out of Arizona into New Mexico at all.

Given the reasoning presented above, along with the geographic, distance, and directional interpretation, it is possible to arrive at a general location that may be the true site of the fabled Lost Adams Diggings. Once this is accomplished, it logically follows that a field investigation should determine if the location possesses any of the characteristics associated with Adams's famous canyon.

It is directly within the realm of possibility, given an application of logic, that the original Lost Adams Diggings could be found in the region of the Arizona–New Mexico border not far from the San Francisco River and the present-day small Arizona town of Clifton.

It is worthwhile to recall that C. A. Shaw noted early on in his relationship with Adams that his partner had a poor sense of direction and distance and had difficulty remembering important landmarks. The Adams-led, Shaw-funded expeditions in search of the diggings got lost on each trip, often several times.

When Adams led his own expeditions independent of Shaw, he had no better luck. During one, he led a group of investors and recruits to a location in northeastern Arizona at least 120 straight-line miles from the Datil Mountains.

Shaw claimed that Chief Nana, in a conversation with a Warm Springs Indian Reservation agent named Cline, spoke of Itsnatahey Canyon and pointed generally toward the east when he did so. That would have placed the location near the present-day town of Clifton. If the location of the canyon of gold were the Datil Mountains, he would have pointed toward the northeast. It can be assumed with confidence that the Apache was more knowledgeable about and experienced with direction than Adams. Nana's statement should carry some weight.

There is yet more evidence that Adams's geographic credibility cannot be accepted. When relating the escape from the canyon with his friend Jack Davidson, Adams said they were found two weeks later by a platoon of US Cavalry. When interviewed years later, Adams said the soldiers carried them to Fort Apache and dropped them off at the post hospital, where they were treated for exhaustion and malnutrition.

The historical record shows that Fort Apache did not exist in 1864. It was designated as a fort by the US government in 1879, fifteen years later. Up until that time, this somewhat remote outpost was called Camp Thomas and had been referred to as such since 1872. Prior to that, it was called Camp Ord, which was established in 1870, six years after Adams and the party of miners arrived at the canyon of gold. Some argue that Adams and Davidson were taken to Fort West, which was, in truth, the closest military installation. Fort West was established in 1863 and lies northwest of Silver City, but in the opposite direction Adams claimed he and Davidson traveled.

According to rancher A. M. Tenny, John Brewer, like Adams, was also apparently inept at recalling and calculating distances and directions. Like Adams, Brewer, in recalling the event twenty-four years later, mentioned that the supply party crossed the Little Colorado River. One can surmise he referred to the river by that name because he heard it from Adams. Similarly, the directions provided by Emil Schaeffer, the German member of the party, to the man who related them to Doc Young were vague, inaccurate, and made little sense. Ultimately, all of the directions provided by the members of the party who were interviewed and quoted—Adams, Schaeffer, and Brewer—proved worthless.

When James B. Gray allegedly found the diggings from which he claimed to have pulled four large nuggets, he was east of the San Carlos Apache Indian Reservation, which would have placed him near the town of Clifton, Arizona, and nowhere near the Datil Mountains.

It is also worth analyzing the account of Jason Baxter. Little in James McKenna's account of Baxter's tales provides any element of comfort relative to his credibility. Baxter's stories seem too good to be true, somewhat like Dobie's. Baxter's revelations about the Lost Adams Diggings have the feel of having been made up and are filled with assumptions, and few, if any, of his statements have ever been verified.

At one point in Baxter's account he spoke of standing on a ridge in the Datil Mountains and spotting the White Mountains of Arizona to the northwest. In fact, the White Mountains are not northwest but west of the Datils. In addition, they are not notably high and would be difficult to spot under the best of conditions from Baxter's alleged position.

Baxter also claimed that from the Datil Mountains he rode toward the west. At one point he said he climbed a ridge, looked to the north, and saw the San Mateo Mountains. In fact, the San Mateo Mountains lie about sixty miles southeast, not north, of the Datils. Someone claiming as much outdoor experience as Baxter should know the difference between north and southeast.

From this same position, Baxter also stated that he traveled in a southerly direction, heading for the northern end of the Mogollon Mountains. The Mogollon range is fifty miles southwest, not south, of the Datils. Once he arrived in the Mogollons, Baxter stated, he struck the headwaters of the "Frisco River just west of Clifton." Again, Baxter's claims lack credibility. The headwaters of the San Francisco River lie over sixty miles northeast of Clifton.

It is also worth mentioning here that while Baxter describes his crossing of the vast Plains of San Augustin on his way to the Datil Mountains, that hugely significant landform—over twelve hundred square miles and too large to miss or ignore—was never mentioned by Adams.

Following a careful examination and analysis of Baxter's tales, it becomes clear that he had no more skill than Adams at interpreting direction and distance. Or, more likely, he fabricated all of it. Therefore, his contributions to the determination of the location of the Lost Adams Diggings must be rejected.

In all the accumulated accounts of the Lost Adams Diggings, there remains little consistency relative to geography, distance, and direction. The many searches for the diggings have extended across a region as large as some eastern states. Various expeditions have covered an estimated twenty thousand square miles in search of the canyon of gold. This suggests that no one had a clue as to the actual location. Mountain ranges identified as the site of the lost canyon have included the Datils, the Mogollons, the San Franciscos, the San Mateos, the Tularosas, the Zunis, and others. Each of these ranges has been explored extensively over the decades, and yet the lost canyon has never been verifiably found. Why? Because it was not located in any of them.

One interesting and perplexing element, however, has re-mained constant with regard to the canyon that may house the lost diggings: the sentinels who allegedly watch over the gold and the canyon.

As related earlier, many have long identified the Datil Mountains of west-central New Mexico as the true location of the Lost Adams Diggings. The selection of this site originated with Bob Lewis, who claimed he found it, stating that he encountered the skeletal remains of men and horses that he presumed were from the Brewer supply party. Jason Baxter subsequently adopted the Datils as the location of the lost canyon of gold, probably having heard Lewis's story. The accounts of these two men were subsequently elaborated on by popular author J. Frank Dobie, who seldom checked on the veracity and credibility of his sources. Dobie's version of the tale of the Lost Adams Diggings was then made available to the public via his book *Apache Gold and Yaqui Silver*, and that location became embedded in the minds of readers and pursuers of lost mines.

Lewis may have found something, but it was certainly not the Lost Adams Diggings. The historical record yields enough evidence to suggest that neither Lewis nor Baxter could be trusted with accurate descriptions or the truth.

Regardless, most treasure hunters and adventurers who went in search of the Lost Adams Diggings concentrated their activities in the Datil Mountains. The overriding question, given a logical analysis of all the evidence available, is why? The probable answer is that they were influenced strongly by Dobie's captivating story and accepted his descriptions at face value, conducting little to no research themselves. Unfortunately for the searchers, Dobie gave too much undeserved credence to the tales offered by Lewis and Baxter. Furthermore, subsequent writers compounded Dobie's errors by repeating what he wrote and performing little to no investigation.

There is another possibility. It can be argued that Adams provided Lewis, as well as others, with erroneous information in order to throw him off the trail. Consider this: We have two men—Adams and Lewis—both searching for the same incredibly rich placer mine in a remote canyon at the same time and in the same general area. Why would Adams give Lewis important locational information that in the long run could cost Adams his gold? It is possible and even probable that Adams sent Lewis off in a direction far from the lost canyon of gold. He may have sent him to the Datil Mountains, a place sufficiently removed from the actual location of the canyon and that, incidentally, Adams never visited.

Lewis, Baxter, Dobie, and a host of subsequent writers provided us with tales. That's all they were—tales, tall ones, accompanied, for the most part, by no logic or truth.

We cannot consider the Datil Mountains as a logical location for the Lost Adams Diggings for yet another reason. In every version of the tale of this lost placer mine, the Indians encountered in and around the canyon were always Apaches. A short distance to the west of Clifton is the San Carlos Apache Indian Reservation. Adams's guide, Gotch Ear, told him that he had visited this canyon while living with a band of Apaches led by Chief Nana. The canyon, called Itsnatahey by Nana, a Warm Springs Apache, was sacred to that particular tribe. The Indians encountered in the canyon by Adams and his party, as well as others who visited or claimed to have visited, were Apaches. There has never been any confusion or doubt about this fact.

The Datil Mountains, located in west-central New Mexico, the range most often associated with the Lost Adams Diggings, lie outside the range of any of the various Apache tribes that roamed and lived in the regions of Arizona and New Mexico, especially the Warm Spring Apaches and Chief Nana. Further, the range lies one hundred miles from Chief Nana's established territory. The Datil Mountains, in truth, were part of the homeland of the Zuni

Indians, not the Apaches. There would have been little reason for the Apache Indians to venture to the Datil Mountains.

Given the above analysis, it becomes unerringly clear where the Lost Adams Diggings are *not* located.

So, the question becomes, Where can Adams's elusive lost canyon of gold be found? On one of his expeditions in search of the lost placer, Adams traveled directly to the San Francisco River valley in southeastern Arizona with none of the confusion that characterized his earlier searches. He was heard to state that he was certain the lost canyon was in this region. Before Adams passed away in September 1886, he told acquaintances that he was convinced that he was finally close to the famous diggings. He made that statement while he was in the San Francisco Mountains near Clifton, Arizona.

Given all the available information, together with an extensive examination of all the evidence, the application of inductive and deductive reasoning, and a thorough study of directions, distances, and the geography involved, one can only conclude that the Lost Adams Diggings are located in the region of the San Francisco Mountains not far from the town of Clifton, Arizona.

✣ 16 ✣

The Question of Mythology

Following the rigid analysis and reconstruction of the original Adams expedition, we remain confronted with a number of elements of the tale of the lost diggings that invite closer examination. In particular, the mythological aspects of the story bear uncomfortably close resemblance to a number of the most prominent treasure tales that have evolved and been handed down over the ages since the dawn of mankind. In other words, a preponderance of the so-called facts related to the Lost Adams Diggings come straight from the pages of traditional mythology. Such a thing demands analysis and criticism and provokes the question: How much of the traditionally accepted version of the Lost Adams Diggings is true and how much is made up?

Much of the history of the western United States, particularly lore about lost mines and buried treasure, is almost certainly myth. The story of the Lost Adams Diggings is almost too perfect. Its resemblance to classical myth should arouse suspicion in anyone who examines it closely. Successful professional treasure hunters recognize these elements right off. Over the generations since Adams and his party encountered the elusive canyon of gold, many have been attracted to and taken in by this compelling tale of adventure, with its quest, secret location, lost fortune, heroes, villains, and more.

Surprisingly, previous researchers never noticed the similarities between the story of the Lost Adams Diggings and so many other quests for gold or wealth. Furthermore, most, if not all, were clearly unacquainted with the common and obvious mythological elements that characterize the story. None of the previous writers looked beyond the myth for the truth. Folklorist and writer J. Frank Dobie was well versed in world mythology, enough so to understand mythic structure and content.

I don't think I am going out on a limb here when I state that Dobie himself altered aspects of the story of the diggings such that it resembled a mythological quest for lost treasure more than it related to a set of truths. In the end, Dobie came up with an amazing tale, one that has resonated throughout North American culture for over a century and a half. In the process, however, he managed to ignore, cover, camouflage, or alter the facts. Writers who followed Dobie were, in turn, seduced by the myth. Who wouldn't be? It is, however, the responsibility of committed researchers, investigators, and writers to peel back the layers of myth and look beneath and beyond them in the hope of discerning the facts. Pursuing this goal can put one in a better position to find the lost canyon and the treasure.

One of America's greatest mythologists was the late Joseph Campbell. A brilliant man and scholar, Campbell had the enviable ability to communicate sometimes complicated concepts to the general public, and he did so with his amazing string of books about mythology. Any serious student of lost mines and buried treasures would do well to become intimate with Campbell's works. In particular, the material that follows derives from his *The Hero with a Thousand Faces* and *The Power of Myth* (with Bill Moyers), as well as *The Writer's Journey* by Christopher Vogler, a book inspired by the works of Campbell that deals with the evolution of stories as influenced by mythology.

The story of the Lost Adams Diggings is almost a textbook myth, containing traditional mythic elements such as (1) the hero,

(2) the herald, (3) the call to adventure, (4) the quest, (5) the crossing of a threshold, (6) the secret door, (7) the presence of sentinels, (8) the test, (9) the ordeal, and (10) the reward.

All stories, says Christopher Vogler, consist of a few common structural elements found universally in myths, as well as in fairy tales, dreams, and many movies. Taken together, they are known as the hero's journey. The patterns one finds in the hero's journey are universal, occurring in every society and every era. Though they differ in their particulars from culture to culture, they are fundamentally the same. These tales reflect not so much the truth as the workings of the human mind. They are psychologically valid and emotionally realistic even when they portray fantastic or impossible events. Nearly everyone feels their appeal.

THE HERO

In the story of the Lost Adams Diggings, the hero is obviously the man called Adams. The hero, as defined by Campbell and Vogler, is willing to sacrifice his own needs on behalf of others, much like a shepherd who sets aside his own agenda to serve his flock. According to Adams's own version, he decided to forego the return to California and the freight company he worked for to lead a party of hopeful, dreaming prospectors and miners to an alleged location that promised wealth in the form of gold.

The dramatic purpose of the hero in mythology is to provide a window into the story for the audience. Indeed, the first and principal narrator of the story of the Lost Adams Diggings is Adams himself. A well-rounded hero, according to Campbell, can be "determined, uncertain, charming, forgetful, impatient, and strong in body but weak in heart." Indeed, throughout his life, from the time he set out with the party of miners for the canyon of gold in 1864 until his death in 1886, Adams manifested all these traits.

At the heart of every hero myth is a confrontation with death in an adventure or confrontation in which the hero may live or die. In the story of the Lost Adams Diggings, our hero faced the threat of death when the Apaches stormed the clearing in which the miners had encamped and slew them all. Adams, the hero, hiding in the nearby brush with a partner, evaded this fate.

In mythology, true heroes experience sacrifice. In Adams's case, he lost not only the gold he had panned and hoarded but also the friends he had made during the journey to the canyon. Adams also sacrificed a certain peace of mind. For years after his return to California, he was unable to sleep because of his constant recollection of the slaughter of his friends by the Apaches. It may be said that Adams also sacrificed his memory. For the remainder of his life, he undertook numerous trips into eastern Arizona and western New Mexico to relocate the lost canyon of gold but was never able to find it. According to Dobie, Adams claimed, "The Apaches made me forget."

THE HERALD

In mythology, the herald often serves to bring the challenge to the hero. Often representative of the coming of significant change, the herald is instrumental in issuing the call to adventure. Heralds have long been necessary in mythology in performing this role. In the story of the Lost Adams Diggings, the herald is clearly Gotch Ear.

The herald serves the psychological function of announcing the need for a change, provides motivation, and gets the story moving. Gotch Ear serves this purpose admirably and in the finest tradition of mythology. He delivers the information that a wealth in gold lies a short journey to the east. Adams and the miners are all in a transitional period in their lives and seeking direction. Gotch

Ear provides knowledge not only of the fortune in gold but of the route that will take them to it.

THE CALL TO ADVENTURE

Gotch Ear, as the herald, issues the call to adventure to our hero and his followers. He is the catalyst that gets the story moving along. This call is tied closely with the synchronicity of circumstances. It follows the arrival in one place of three different, yet important elements of the story: Adams, the miners, and Gotch Ear. These coincidental occurrences take on meaning only after the call is issued.

In mythology, the call to adventure is often associated with temptation. The temptation can take a variety of forms: love, success, power, or wealth. In this case, the temptation is the gold that lies yonder, promising to make each of the participants wealthy beyond his wildest imaginings. The call to adventure can sometimes take the form of opportunity. In the case of Adams and the miners, the prospect of finding gold and growing wealthy is far more appealing than any of their other options.

THE QUEST

Most myths involve a quest. The hero starts at Point A and sets out for Point B, the location where he will find what he seeks. In our story, the hero, along with his companions and the herald, start out from near the Pima village located not far from Gila Bend, Arizona. Point B is, of course, the canyon of gold. As with most mythical tales, the journey from Point A to point B is beset with obstacles, many of which have the potential to dissuade the journeyers and cause them to turn back. In Adams's case, obstacles took the form of mountain ranges to cross and rivers to ford, as well as days on end of tedious travel on foot and horseback. Added to these was the threat of Indian attack. The promise of wealth to be gained at Point B, however, offset any hardships encountered along the journey.

CROSSING THE THRESHOLD

In mythology, the hero eventually arrives and stands before the first of potentially several thresholds that he must cross. The hero and his followers have arrived in a kind of no-man's-land. None of them have ever been here before, and they find themselves in a realm of the unknown. Further, attack by Apaches, as Gotch Ear reminds them, can occur at any moment. In fact, at this point they must determine whether to continue or return. They are in what Campbell called the "world between worlds." There is a sense of the presence of other beings, other forces, guarding the way to the treasure they seek. A decision must be made.

THE SECRET DOOR

In the story of the Lost Adams Diggings, the threshold is represented by what Dobie called the "secret door." Adams and the miners, led by Gotch Ear, arrived at a "palisaded wall." The confused miners thought they would have to scale the wall to reach their destination, but Gotch Ear stepped forward and soon "passed behind a boulder that, from a short distance as well as from afar, seemed to be part of the bluff." Behind the boulder was the so-called secret door for which so many questing for the Lost

Adams Diggings have searched. The secret door was, according to description, a narrow opening into the canyon that was their destination.

The concept of the secret door is common to dozens, if not hundreds, of the world's myths. Mythology is filled with secret entrances to forbidden places. In our story, the secret door serves as a portal, the beginning of the path that leads to the gold the men seek but also to a place held sacred and occupied by Apaches.

In mythology, secret doors and secret passages often operate as plot elements or as part of the setting. They are also commonly used in traditional and contemporary fiction and film. One of the most famous secret doors was the one in the tale "Ali Baba and the Forty Thieves." Beyond that door lay a vault filled with precious silks, gold, silver, and other treasures. Secret doors and secret passageways commonly occur in the myths of the Middle East, Egypt, India, Germany, Denmark, Sweden, and Norway.

In the story of the Lost Adams Diggings, Gotch Ear led Adams and the miners through the secret door and into the canyon. From this point on, their lives would be changed dramatically and forever. This scenario is not much different from the tortuous trail that led to the legendary Shangri-La or the journey to Neverland led by Peter Pan.

In the story of the Lost Adams Diggings, the presence of a secret door, while certainly adding a mythic and compelling dimension to the tale, was most likely contrived.

Once in the canyon, a mysterious, exciting world filled with the promise of wealth, Adams and the miners will be subjected to a test, a trial, if you will. On entering the canyon they are now clearly in a special world, a realm far different from the ordinary one in which they live. They have been told of the great fortune they will find there and alerted to the ever-present danger in the form of the Indians. They are filled with anticipation—and dread.

SENTINELS

Once the threshold is crossed, the hero often encounters threshold guardians, which can pose obstacles to the quest. Threshold guardians in mythology are the lieutenants or mercenaries of the main villain. In our story, the main villain is clearly Chief Nana. The threshold guardians take the form of sentinels, members of the tribe over which Nana holds command. The sentinels serve as guards against access to a special place. In this case, the special place is the sacred ground of the Indians.

THE TEST

In mythology, the hero often undergoes a trial, or a series of trials and challenges, meant to prepare him for greater ordeals ahead. Adams, who by now has assumed the role of group leader, has faced a number of smaller challenges. Because of the oncoming winter, he decides it is imperative they have some shelter and organizes the construction of a cabin. He decides that all the gold harvested should be placed in a communal chamber and divided up among the men when they leave the canyon at some future date. He organizes an expedition to acquire needed supplies and provisions. He instructs the miners, following a warning from Apache chief Nana, not to venture above the waterfall into the sacred and forbidden realm of the canyon. When the Apaches attack and kill the miners, Adams, along with partner Jack Davidson, confronts the supreme test: survival.

In mythology, enemies or rivals often test the hero. In this case, the rivals are the Apaches. The miners have encroached on their land. The newcomers have camped close to the Indians' ceremonial grounds and are hunting the wild game so important to the Apaches. Nana, on learning from Adams that the miners will depart in a reasonable time, agrees to allow the intruders to remain in the canyon. When the miners violate Nana's restriction relative to venturing above the falls, the rivals become enemies. This violation changes everything for the miners.

The Apaches first attack the supply party on its return to the canyon, killing most of the participants. Then they attack the miners, killing them and burning down the cabin. Most of the miners do not survive. Adams and Davidson, who had been some distance away from the cabin at the onset of the attack, observe the killing and scalping. When the time is appropriate, they flee the canyon on horseback. They carry no food, no water, and no firearms. As in virtually all hero myths, Adams now confronts his greatest ordeal.

THE ORDEAL

Joseph Campbell writes that the secret of the ordeal in mythology is that the hero must die so that he can be reborn. In every story, the hero faces death or something like it. In our story, Adams faces death at the hands of the marauding Apaches. While he escapes, some part of him does, in fact, die. His life, as he has lived it up to this point, is over, and what follows is a complete symbolic rebirth.

The hero does not simply come face to face with death and return home. He is transformed. The ordeal, which can be likened to a crisis, is the point in myths, and in our story, at which hostile forces are in the tensest state of opposition. No one—and Adams is a good example of this relative to his contact with the Apaches—can endure an experience this close to actual death without being changed in some manner. Sometimes things have to get worse in order to get better, and the worst that has happened thus far in our story is the Indian attack and the slaying of the miners. An ordeal, or crisis, however frightening to the hero, is sometimes the only way back to recovery or victory.

The word "crisis" comes from a Greek term that means "to separate." In Japanese, it is written with two characters that together mean "danger plus opportunity." A crisis, therefore, is an event that separates the two halves of the story. After crossing this zone, which is often "the borderland of death," explains Vogler, "the hero is literally or metaphorically reborn and nothing will ever be the same for him."

Witnessing the death of his comrades is just the beginning of our hero's ordeal. If he remains in the canyon, he will surely be found and dispatched in a similar manner. He must escape. The escape is simply a continuation of Adams's ordeal. On fleeing the canyon in the company of Davidson, he becomes engaged in a continuing fight for survival. After retrieving a gold nugget he had earlier secreted and placing it in his pocket, he steals away in silence in the dark of night. Adams and Davidson retrace as best they can remember the route they had taken to the canyon. They travel only at night for fear of being spotted. They refrain from shooting game for meat lest the sound betray their presence. While one sleeps, the other stands guard. They eat acorns, piñon nuts, and other food found in the wild. They finally kill one of their horses for meat. They drink water from where it has gathered in rock depressions.

Six days after leaving the canyon, our hero and his companion are weary, and their shoes are coming apart. At one point during their return journey, they spot Indians and are forced to hide. On the thirteenth day they encounter several horsemen, troopers of the US Cavalry, and reveal themselves. The two men are taken, according to Adams, to Fort Apache.

At the fort Adams spends several sleepless nights trying to recover from his ordeal. But it is not over. He is awakened one night by the sound of five Indian scouts riding by his tent. Adams claims to recognize two of them as members of Chief Nana's war party that had killed the miners. Minutes after obtaining a pistol, Adams shoots and kills two of the Indians. For this deed, he is charged with murder and placed in the guardhouse to await trial. Two nights later, he escapes, steals a horse, and flees. Weeks later he arrives at his home in California, where he is reunited with his wife and three children. Finally, this part of Adams's ordeal is over, or so it seems.

THE REWARD

The concept of an ultimate reward is another important aspect of mythology. Following the ordeal, the hero revels in having survived death. This triumph may be fleeting, but for the time being, the hero savors its pleasures.

Reward, the aftermath of the ordeal, can take many shapes and purposes. Adams's immediate rewards were associated with his survival and his return from the special world of the canyon to the ordinary world of his homeland and the embrace of loved ones.

Once our hero has achieved his reward, his journey comes to an end. In essence, all of the elements of the story of the Lost Adams Diggings, as interpreted by Dobie and others, have come full circle, and our hero is safe at home. It is entirely noteworthy that this tale follows the pattern of many of the world's greatest myths. Is this a coincidence? Or did this story, as time passed, assume the color and texture of myth as it was told and retold hundreds of times.

As a professional treasure hunter who researches, investigates, deconstructs, analyzes, and reconstructs such tales in an attempt to derive the truth, I have five decades of dealing with the mythological elements of such stories. It is my job, then, to identify these fanciful components of a treasure tale or legend, peel back the layers of myth, and determine what remains. In many cases, tales and legends of lost mines and buried treasures are simply stories with no basis in fact whatsoever. Many of them qualify as good yarns, entertaining and compelling, but fiction nonetheless.

In the case of the Lost Adams Diggings, the myth is based on and has evolved from an actual event. After researching the story for more than forty years, I come away with the notion that events actually transpired in a manner similar to the way they have been presented to the reading public for the past century or so. I am also convinced, as a result of deep and intense immersion in this tale, as well as intimate personal experience with treasure hunting in general and hunting for the Lost Adams Diggings in particular, that much of what we have come to associate with the story never happened.

This observation is in no way an indictment of Adams. I am convinced that Adams told the truth about his adventure as best as he could remember it. The blame for the coloring, exaggerations, and layering of mythological elements for the sake of the story, not the truth, lies primarily with Dobie and secondarily with all who followed him. Dobie was a master storyteller. He knew exactly what he was doing when he embroidered the story of the Lost Adams Diggings with mythological elements. In the end, Dobie gave us what he intended: a great story, one that has endured and attracted thousands, perhaps tens of thousands, to the search for this amazing lost canyon of gold.

None of the subsequent writers of books and articles have proven as adept as Dobie in constructing or even researching a story. A cursory examination of subsequent publications about the Lost Adams Diggings reveals that the authors did little more than simply repeat, in one form or another, what Dobie gave us.

Nonetheless the tale of the Lost Adams Diggings remains a wonderful adventure story, one with a hero, danger, and a magnificent quest for wealth. It is a story that will remain with us for a long time as a result of the masterful mythologizing layered onto it by Dobie. But the story is not a complete truth, only a partial one. Yet even that partial truth is enough to set the adventurous soul off in search of this amazing location of gold.

That is precisely what I did. The following pages will share my decades-long research and analysis of the story of the Lost Adams Diggings, my own personal search for the location, and ultimately my rediscovery of the site. In many ways, this adventure contains the elements of a mythological quest itself.

PART IV

The Rediscovery of the Lost Adams Diggings

✢ 17 ✢

The Call

I have been a professional treasure hunter for over five decades. I have studied, researched, and searched for famous and unknown lost treasures throughout the United States and Mexico. I have had a number of successes and numerous failures—failures only in the sense that the lost treasures sought were not found. No expedition, however, was a complete loss, for each one provided some level of adventure, danger, and suspense, as well as important experience and knowledge. I learned a lot about locating lost treasures by searching for them, spending considerable time in the field alone and in the company of other professionals. It was constant on-the-job training, so to speak. Each expedition was different, offering unique challenges and rewards.

Most professional treasure hunters prefer anonymity. There are reasons for this. Competition to find a certain lost treasure is not unusual in this odd business, so it serves no purpose to let others, treasure hunters and non–treasure hunters alike, know precisely what one is up to. In addition, given my own philosophy and approach to discovery and recovery, practically everything I do is illegal. Therefore, the fewer people who know about what I am doing as it relates to searching for lost mines and buried treasures, the better. For many years, members of my own family had no specific knowledge of my activities during my expeditions. My level of anonymity, however, has been altered somewhat by the publication of more than thirty books devoted to tales of lost mines and buried treasures as well as a memoir (*Treasure Hunter: Caches, Curses, and Deadly Confrontations*) recounting some of my most memorable expeditions. In addition, my name became far better known than I had anticipated after I appeared on national television and consulted for motion pictures. For the most part, however, I attempt to fly well under the radar, but I still have to be careful.

After so many years of researching, investigating, reconstructing, and conducting expeditions in search of lost treasures, famous and not so famous, as well as writing numerous books about the subject, I have learned that the problem with most published accounts—and it is a significant one—is that they are written by men and women who are not professional treasure hunters. In virtually every account I have ever read, the writer doesn't have the foggiest notion of what is involved in a search for a treasure or a mine and ultimately manifests little or no experience in such things other than repeating what someone else has already written and published.

This problem of repetition is significant relative to the Lost Adams Diggings story. Of the countless magazine and newspaper articles and handful of books on the topic, none of the published material that I have seen manifests any degree of professionalism or skill in terms of research, analysis, logic, or even writing. As a result, nearly all the published material related to the Lost Adams Diggings lacks quality, credibility, and, importantly, accuracy. With little difficulty, most of the legend can be traced back to J. Frank Dobie's 1928 publication of *Apache Gold and Yaqui Silver*. Dobie's version, though a thrilling and captivating read, is replete with inaccuracies and exaggerations by his own admission. Since then, dozens, if not hundreds, of men and women have, to one degree or another, simply repeated what Dobie wrote. So the task for the serious researcher is to separate the legend from the fact, the lore from the truth.

Since it was clear early on that my books were based on considerable research, investigation, and personal involvement, they caught the attention of many who regarded me, rightly or wrongly, as a source of important information. Magazines asked me to write the "true" story of one lost mine or another. I was contacted by publishers who wanted to produce authoritative books on lost mines and buried treasures. And I was, and still am, contacted by television and film production companies to consult on or be involved with features and documentaries on these same subjects. In addition, I am often contacted by individuals who want me to write the story of their discovery of some lost treasure.

I receive e-mails and telephone calls on the order of three to four times per week from people wanting information I might possess regarding a particular lost treasure as well as from those who claim to have found one. Of all the claims of discoveries I have received over the years—and there have been many—none has ever held up under investigation.

One afternoon in 1990, however, I received a call from a stranger who wanted to talk about a famous lost mine—the Lost Adams Diggings. His voice and demeanor over the telephone were pleasant, and as I had a few minutes to spare between projects, I told him I would listen. It was the beginning of one of the strangest quests for lost treasure I have ever been involved with.

The caller introduced himself as Jim Peterson and said he was living at the time in Dolores, Colorado, a few miles north of Cortez, near the southwestern corner of the state. The caller proceeded to tell me he was acquainted with a chapter from a book and several articles I had written pertaining to the famous Lost Adams Diggings. He also said he had spent several weeks searching for that very same elusive canyon of gold. He was convinced that I had presented most of the details regarding the lost placer mine accurately except for one important part. I asked him what that was, and he replied, the actual location of the canyon.

I'm very open-minded about such things and never consider that I might have the final word on any given subject. I told Mr. Peterson I would be happy to listen to whatever he wanted to tell me about the diggings and their location and hoped that I might learn something important.

Peterson spent the next few minutes explaining his own research on and experiences with the Lost Adams Diggings. He also spoke in detail about his efforts to locate the placer mine and about the several trips he had taken to the region. He explained that he found everything where, according to the legend, it was supposed to be: the zigzag canyon, the ruins of an old log cabin, the stone hearth, the hidden compartment, the waterfall, the Apache campground, and, most importantly, gold. All in all, we had a pleasant conversation. I was inclined to dispute little about what Peterson told me, but he remained vague about the exact location of his discovery. Since I had already eliminated the traditionally accepted location—the Datil Mountains region of west-central New Mexico—I decided to see if I could trip up Peterson by asking if that was where he had concentrated his efforts. He replied that the Datil Mountains could never be seriously considered as the location of the famous mine by anyone who spent any time conducting any kind of significant research. Peterson scored some points with me with that answer.

After another fifteen minutes of conversation, I asked Peterson his reasons for telling me about his alleged rediscovery of the mine. He said that virtually all accounts of the journey of the Adams party to the lost canyon, as well as other aspects of the tale including subsequent searches, were in error, and he wanted to set the record straight. He said it was time the truth was told, and he asked me if I would consider writing it.

I explained to Peterson that I could not undertake such a project based on his word alone. I would have to see the canyon with my own eyes to ascertain that all the appropriate landmarks were in place and that the geography of the location that Peterson selected was consistent with my own research and calculations, as well as with aspects of the legend. I would also need to see some gold panned from the stream. If Peterson's contentions did not agree with my analysis, I would need to be persuaded to continue with the experiment. Peterson agreed that I needed to visit the canyon and that that was the only honest way to undertake the project. He said he was prepared to meet with me, get to know me, and see if I could be trusted enough to be led to the famous diggings.

I informed Peterson that I was unable to get away from my home base for several months as a result of book deadlines, speaking engagements, scheduled treasure-hunting expeditions, and other obligations. I did promise to stay in touch and that, when possible, we would work out a time to meet and continue our dialog. In the meantime, Peterson wrote me several letters detailing his ventures into what he claimed was Adams's lost canyon of gold.

Time passed, and in 1992 I had some speaking engagements in Arizona and New Mexico, one of which was not far from Peterson's place of residence near Dolores. I wrote to him and, following a brief exchange of letters, made arrangements to meet him at his home. On my arrival days later, the two of us got down to business right away, with the subject of the Lost Adams Diggings dominating the discussion. I made several more attempts to determine if Peterson was correct in his claim of locating the famous lost mine and again asked a number of leading questions designed to trip him up. I was unsuccessful because he appeared to have all the correct answers.

I listened, patiently and attentively, as he related his own experiences searching for the legendary placer mine. He had been to the location several times, he said. In his opinion, all the landmarks and landscape features he mentioned were consistent with the accepted versions of the Lost Adams Diggings. He described them in detail. When he finished, I asked Peterson if he could tell me the location. He again stated he would not. I explained again that I would not be able to write anything about it unless I could verify his claim personally. I explained that I needed to see the canyon and observe all the landmarks and the evidence. It was the only honest and responsible thing to do. I also told him I needed to find gold in the famous little stream that wound through the canyon, a process I believed to be the ultimate proof, assuming all the other elements could be verified.

Peterson said he would not tell me where the canyon of gold was located but would take me there. I agreed to the proposition. Our schedules were such that we could not undertake the journey during that particular visit; it would have to wait for another time. We agreed to begin making plans for such an expedition.

Before leaving Peterson, I asked him if he could tell me how he had determined the location of the Lost Adams Diggings and decided to visit and investigate the precise canyon he told me about. I was in for a surprise and a shock, because his explanation was bizarre and unbelievable, making me doubt that Peterson knew what he was talking about. I came close to thanking him for his time, excusing myself, and walking out of his house. The good manners I was raised with, however, dictated that I hear him out.

Peterson told me he had "witched" the site for the first time in 1986. "Witching" for something is synonymous with "dowsing," a method whereby an individual, using an apparatus such as a divining rod or a forked tree limb, searches for underground water; some witchers employ a vial of water dangling from a chain or cord. I have seen some witchers use two straightened-out coat hangers with success.

Over the years I have met a number of men who claimed to be able to witch, or dowse, for minerals such as gold and silver. I have listened to numerous accounts of such accomplishments. Though I have observed a number of successes related to dowsing for water, I have never personally observed anyone succeed in dowsing for minerals or metal.

When it comes to witching/dowsing for minerals, I am a skeptic. In the past men have approached me about participating in one or more of my treasure-hunting expeditions, claiming skills in witching for whatever mineral I was seeking. Most of them insisted they could witch a treasure site from as much as a mile away, perhaps more.

Thus, I subjected each one who came to me to a test I devised. I would hide a gold or silver object nearby—a coin or ingot—and ask them to locate it via the dowsing process. Every one of them failed, and I was left with the notion that this process did not work. I am not stating here that it is impossible; I am merely explaining that when put to the test, none of the claimants I encountered succeeded. I am still waiting to be convinced.

I asked Peterson to explain the mechanics of his witching process so that I might better understand it. He stated that he employed a "dowsing instrument." His instrument consisted of a ring composed of gold and silver and a small magnet, all placed in a leather pouch that had been "saturated with a solution of mercury to offset . . . surrounding radio interference." This pouch hung from a short cord. Peterson would hold the end of the cord between forefinger and thumb, allowing the pouch to dangle, waiting for it to react. Peterson said the pouch would begin to "move and point." The pouch did not so much point as become oriented toward an object. He would follow the directional orientation until he arrived at what he was seeking. In this manner, he claimed, he has found gold, silver, and other metals.

Jim Peterson's discovery of the Lost Adams Diggings via the witching process is even stranger. Years earlier, at his farm in Allison, seventy-five miles to the southeast and near the border with New Mexico, Peterson, using his instrument, dowsed an Arizona state map. He claimed he received a signal immediately. He said it was the strongest signal he had ever received. He also stated that the signals were the most powerful when the location was associated with death. His instrument touched the map at a location near the town of Clifton.

Several weeks after the dowsing session, Peterson, in the company of his two sons, David and Vern, drove from Allison to the general area indicated on the map. He purchased a topographic map at a forestry service station and witched it again. Back in the vehicle, Peterson then drove to within one mile of the precise location he dowsed on the cartograph.

Unable to contain myself, I told Peterson I did not believe such a thing was possible and that the very notion of dowsing, from a piece of paper, the location of a lost gold mine three hundred miles to the southeast of where he sat was too absurd to contemplate. When I was convinced that things could not get weirder, Peterson told me an amazing story that involved a serious accident that dramatically affected him and its vitally important aftermath. As he related his story, my doubts only increased, and I told him so. In the end, however, he provided verification of everything he stated.

On April 8, 1978, Jim Peterson had an accident that changed his life. He was a truck driver for the Les Calkins Trucking Company. On that fateful day, he bade his wife, Shirley, good-bye, left his home in Elk Grove, California, and drove to a depot where he picked up a cement truck. After the truck was filled with cement from the Kaiser Cement Company, he proceeded to a construction site. As Peterson approached his destination, a portion of the road caved in, and the truck rolled over. Peterson's head struck a steel box in the cab. He was rendered unconscious and suffered a severe concussion. When he regained his senses in a hospital days later, he did not recognize his family. He was fifty-one years old.

In addition to the concussion, Peterson suffered injuries to his lower back and neck. He also experienced episodes of extreme dizziness. A diagnosis by a doctor named Hambley suggested that the sudden impact and shock of the accident could have caused damage to the labyrinth (associated with the inner ear and related to balance). Peterson was seen by a Dr. Clift, who wrote that the patient "had a post-traumatic syndrome of head, neck, back, and hip pain" and suffered from "spinal aches." On May 1, 1979, Peterson was treated by a Dr. Lamond, who confirmed the two earlier diagnoses.

Beginning in July 1981, Peterson began seeing Dr. James A. Peal, a Stockton, California, psychiatrist. In a filed report, Peal noted that Peterson's accident had left him with "spells of disturbances of consciousness which caused him to be afraid to drive." Dizziness and headaches accompanied these spells, and sometimes the patient fell down during such episodes. In addition, Peterson suffered from depression. According to Peal the accident had caused "anxiety neurosis." Records show that Peterson had monthly sessions with Dr. Peal from July 1981 through May 1982.

Going into greater detail, Peal stated that Peterson suffered from "flashes" during which he saw "strange color combinations of blues and greens that blend into everything else." At the same time, Peterson experienced a sudden and severe headache and fell to the ground, unconscious. When he awoke, the headaches remained for a time. According to Peal and Peterson, during these flashes the patient had "unusual psychological experiences." Via these flashes, Peterson received "information and insight such that he is, or has been, able to predict world events, local events, and events which happen to individuals and countries." The flashes, according to Peterson, came as a vision. He referred to them as "insights."

Peterson's first vision occurred in September 1978. According to Dr. Peal, "in these visions [Peterson] is able to see the events actually happen." During this September vision, Peterson "saw" a severe earthquake in Iran in which over sixteen hundred people perished. A few days later, television stations and newspapers around the world reported on the Iranian earthquake. It was exactly as Peterson had described it.

During subsequent months, Peterson predicted earthquakes in Santa Barbara, San Diego, and Palm Desert, California, as well as one in Mexico. Regarding the Palm Desert quake, Peterson's prediction was off by only twenty minutes. In early December

1980, he predicted the assassination attempt on President Ronald Reagan, which happened four months later. Peterson also accurately predicted the assassination of Egyptian president Anwar Sadat two weeks before it occurred on October 6, 1981, in Cairo.

During another flash, Peterson "saw" ships of the Royal Navy going to the Falkland Islands in the Atlantic Ocean off the east coast of the southern tip of South America prior to the onset of that war. In addition, he "saw" that the Argentine navy had Russian naval equipment. Related to the same war, Peterson experienced "flashes that the U.S. Central Intelligence Agency warned President Reagan and General Alexander Haig to delay the Falkland situation until Britain got armed." All of these flashes occurred weeks before American citizens had any inkling of events in the Falkland Islands.

All of Peterson's predictions came to him during his flashes. They were disturbing, causing him to feel "tense and anxious" because he felt he needed to warn people but didn't know how to go about it. He decided he would alert his local newspaper, which did not take him seriously until it became clear that he was amazingly accurate in his predictions.

A newspaper reporter also noted Peterson's predictions and started writing about them. Every prediction came true. His wife began calling a Sacramento television station with information about Jim's insights because she thought they were important. The station reported on Peterson's predictions with some regularity. When a reporter for the television station named Bill Harvey called Peterson and said he would like to come to his home and interview him, Shirley grew concerned because they lived in a poor part of town and had little in the way of possessions; she expressed embarrassment at having such an environment presented on television. Respecting Shirley's wishes, Peterson refused the interview. A short time later he decided not to call the station with his predictions anymore.

I subsequently learned that Peterson had predicted the earth-quake that generated the giant tsunami that devastated a portion of Indonesia. Years before it occurred, he also predicted Hurricane Katrina and the subsequent devastation of the city of New Orleans. Curiously, Peterson even predicted it would be named "Katrina."

In summary, it was apparent from visiting with Jim Peterson and reading the official medical reports related to his condition that he possessed an unusual psychic sense bordering on the super-natural. By comparison, his claim that he had dowsed the location of the Lost Adams Diggings on a map in his home seemed almost trivial.

Peterson's baffling and amazing abilities aside, I remained unconvinced. I told him I would still have to see the lost canyon of gold for myself. There was no other way I would write about it. He said he would make that happen, and we began to formulate plans to get together sometime in the future to undertake a journey to the canyon.

⚜ 18 ⚜

Journey to the Canyon

In 1994, I was booked for an appearance in Tucson, Arizona. When Jim Peterson learned of this, he wrote and asked if we could meet in Morenci, Arizona. Morenci is a company town built around the copper-mining activity operated at the time by the Phelps Dodge Corporation and located 110 miles northeast of Tucson and immediately north of Clifton. I agreed and told him I could be there at a certain time on a certain day. He provided directions to the company store where, he said, he would buy me lunch. I found his selection of the location to meet an odd and interesting one, since my own research suggested the possibility that Adams's lost canyon of gold was likely located not far from there.

After leaving Tucson, I drove to Morenci and met Peterson at the front door of the company store (now a chain grocery enterprise). He was accompanied by his wife, Shirley. Peterson ordered lunch for us: baloney sandwiches, potato chips, and Cokes. While we ate, we discussed the Lost Adams Diggings. Once again, I posed questions in an attempt to determine whether there was the possibility of a hoax. In every case, Peterson answered my questions appropriately.

Referring to the maze of mountain ranges found in that part of Arizona, I commented that a search for the lost canyon of gold could be challenging. I also related that, according to my own calculations and reckoning, I was convinced the Lost Adams

Diggings were somewhere in the vicinity. Peterson regarded me for a moment, then said, "They are."

All that was left, then, I told him, was for him to tell me where the canyon was located so that I could make arrangements to return to the area and explore it for myself or, if he preferred, in his company. Peterson replied that he could do better than that. He told me he was going to take me directly to the legendary canyon as soon as we finished lunch.

"It's that easy?" I asked. He replied that it was. We completed our meal and walked out of the store. He said he would leave Shirley in his truck and asked if it was all right to take mine. I assented. He escorted Shirley to his vehicle, an older-model pickup with a weathered camper on the back. I waited for him by my truck, parked only fifty feet away. After he said good-bye to his wife and approached, I expressed concern about leaving Shirley alone in the cab of his truck. He explained that she was used to it, always insisting on waiting for him while he explored. Besides, he said, we won't be gone very long. When I asked him how far it was to the canyon, he replied that it was about ten minutes away.

We pulled out of the parking lot of the company store and onto Arizona Highway 191 and headed north. Within seconds I was steering my vehicle along the route that wound through one of the largest copper mines and processing facilities in the world. At least twice I was forced to stop and wait for huge ore haulers to cross the highway from the mines on the east side of the road to some location on the west. A few minutes after passing the limits of the mining-related activity, Peterson suggested that I slow down because we were going to pull off the road a short distance ahead.

Responding to Peterson's directions, I eased off the highway, into the mouth of a canyon, and onto a level space. Peterson told me this was where he usually parked. Nearby were the remains of an old corral. We climbed out of the truck. I shouldered a small backpack containing a canteen filled with water, a camera, and a notepad.

Standing at the mouth of the canyon, Peterson pointed toward a location across the road and at least one hundred yards away. It was a relatively flat area and manifested the remains of a small vegetable garden. He informed me it was the location of the pumpkin patch often referred to by Adams and others. Peterson drew my attention to a narrow, spring-fed stream that irrigated the plot. It would be hard to prove that it was the original pumpkin patch after the passage of a century and a half, but it appeared to be an ideal site for such.

"Where to?" I asked Peterson after he hoisted his own backpack.

"We're here," he said. "This is the canyon."

I looked around, anticipation rising, expectations holding steady. I noted the rather narrow canyon and the healthy tree growth, the hum of insects, the sounds of birds, and the shallow creek running down the center. I turned back to Peterson and watched as he strapped a leather belt with a holster around his waist. He then checked a .44-caliber revolver, making certain it was loaded. Satisfied, he placed it in the holster.

"Expecting trouble?" I asked.

"Rattlesnakes," he replied. "Lots of them. Also black bear and mountain lion."

He proceeded to walk up the canyon. I followed. I saw no signs stating the canyon was posted or that it was private property. I asked Peterson about this, and he told me that he thought a rancher owned or leased a portion of the canyon. He said a short distance farther up, it became the property of either the US Forest Service or the Bureau of Land Management. I wasn't certain, but I suspected that it might be part of the Apache-Sitgreaves National Forest, which covered a large swath of land in the area. Subsequent examination of a map revealed that it was indeed Forest Service land.

We hiked up the canyon along a seldom-used trail that paralleled the shallow, narrow stream. Tall trees provided shade. During this portion of the hike, Peterson told me he had visited the canyon for the first time in 1986, following the "pull" of his vision from the dowsing. "I was just led here," he said.

After one hundred yards I called a halt and addressed Peterson. If this is the correct location, I said, then the stream we are walking next to must be the one from which Adams and the miners panned the gold. He said I was correct and informed me that it was called Chesser Creek and the canyon through which we hiked was named Chesser Gulch.

I told Peterson I wanted to stop and have a closer look at the stream and its contents. As I dipped my hand into the water and retrieved a small amount of gravel to examine, Peterson said I was not likely to find much, if anything. When I asked why, he said the stream, at least this lower end of it, had been panned out. I asked him to explain.

Peterson said that not only did Adams and his miners remove a great deal of gold from the stream, but subsequent heavy placer mining activity depleted most of what was left. He explained that during the construction of Highway 191, a number of the workers would take their lunch into the canyon and relax and eat in the cool shade. During one of these lunch breaks, one of them was washing his utensils in the stream when he spotted some color glinting on the bottom. When he retrieved the object, he was surprised and delighted to discover it was a tiny gold nugget. During lunch the next day, all the members of the road crew entered the canyon and panned for gold, harvesting a surprisingly large amount. Before long, they quit their jobs with the road construction company and spent all their time panning for gold up and down the stream. Some of the men even set up camp in the canyon, leaving on oc- casion to travel into Morenci or Clifton to replenish food and supplies. Peterson said that many of the road construction workers told friends and relatives about the possibility of harvesting impres- sive amounts of gold from the stream, and before long there were as many as sixty men panning gold from the location for weeks on end. Road construction related to Highway 191 was halted for weeks until more workers could be hired.

In addition, over time others found gold in the stream. On weekends, men came from as far away as Tucson to pan for gold. During one trip to the canyon, Peterson spotted a man panning in a section of Chase Creek alongside Highway 191 and about forty yards downstream from the canyon entrance. (Chesser Creek flows into Chase Creek at the mouth of the canyon.) When he went to speak with him, the man showed Peterson a small mason jar one-quarter filled with gold nuggets he said he had panned during the previous two hours.

As we continued up the canyon, Peterson in the lead, I perceived a certain zigzag pattern like that referred to numerous times by Adams and others. I mentioned it to Peterson, and he nodded his head. As I followed, I cast glances along both sides of the trail, ever wary of rattlesnakes. I mentioned to Peterson that a .44 seemed like a bit of overkill for reptiles. He replied that it was the only revolver he owned.

Presently we came to a bend and veered toward the right. The canyon floor opened up a bit, providing a relatively extensive level area with grasses filling in the space. A short distance ahead I spotted another corral—weathered, long unused, and in a state of disrepair. It consisted of poles set in the ground every eight feet or so, with juniper branches strung together vertically with wire. Peterson was standing still several paces ahead of me. He had stopped on the trail and was staring straight ahead. When I caught up to him, I looked in the direction of his gaze and just beyond the corral saw a crude log cabin. It was constructed of logs, planks, and rocks and covered by a tin roof.

Peterson pointed at it and said, "That's where the Adams party built their cabin."

I paused a couple of seconds to let this soak in. Unable to contain myself, I pointed out to Peterson that the Adams cabin was destroyed by fire well over a century earlier and that the one we were looking at was probably only sixty to seventy years old, complete with a tin roof. Peterson smiled and explained.

He pointed out that the area we were standing in was the only location in the canyon wide enough to serve as a setting for a cabin and a corral in which to pen the horses brought by Adams and the miners. Furthermore, there was a certain amount of decent grass for the grazing of horses in the flat areas here adjacent to the stream. The cabin we were looking at was constructed, he said, by a rancher named Chesser during the 1930s and used by his Mexican ranch hands while they were working in this area. This cabin, he said, while pointing to the extant structure, was built in this location atop the site of the Adams party cabin.

On two earlier visits to this location, Peterson explained, he dug several holes and shallow trenches around the more recent cabin as well as in the dirt floor inside the structure. At a depth of eight inches, he found a layer of charcoal that appeared at every site he excavated. He suggested that the charcoal represented the remains of the cabin constructed by the Adams party. I pointed out that the charcoal could have come from a forest fire sometime in the past. Peterson said he suspected such a thing was possible, but with each hole he excavated he found more evidence of an earlier cabin at this site. He uncovered the remains of what he suspected were roof poles, about three inches thick. He found pieces of notched logs. He found arrowheads, one of which was embedded into a piece of log. Peterson also found several bones that, though never positively identified, he believed were human.

We entered the cabin. It was approximately sixteen feet by fourteen feet. Inside I spotted the remains of two sets of rusted bedsprings along with a wreck of a cast iron stove, a chair, a table, and some discarded broken and rusted tools. At one end of the cabin was a rock fireplace and what remained of a chimney.

Staring at the rock hearth, I asked Peterson if he reckoned it had been constructed atop the one in which the Adams party had secreted their gold. Peterson smiled at me again, pointed to the structure, and said, "That is the same hearth that the Adams party built. It was not destroyed by the fire in 1864. This newer cabin that we are standing in now was built around that old hearth."

"If that's true," I said, "then it should be a simple matter of finding the secret chamber."

Peterson said there was not one but two secret compartments. He indicated I should follow him outside. We walked around the cabin and stood next to the rock hearth. Removing a large stone, he pointed into the back of the rock structure at an added receptacle, one capable of storing dozens of pouches of gold nuggets. The hearth and associated chimney had seen considerable weathering and degradation over the past century and more. Further, Peterson explained, when he found the secret chamber a few years earlier by pulling out some of the rocks, it was empty; someone had gotten to it before he did.

Peterson then showed me a large flagstone that covered the space adjacent to and slightly beneath the hearth. This was the hidden location referred to in the Lost Adams Diggings literature where the miners had placed more of their gold nuggets. He pulled the stone and exposed the space below. It was considerably larger than the chamber located at the back of the hearth, and it too was empty. Somebody, or somebodies, had found the gold stored here long ago and removed it. There existed no clues relative to who it might have been, but Peterson suggested that perhaps it was one of the surviving miners who eventually returned to the location. When Peterson first encountered the secret compartment below the hearth, he found only the remains of an old rusted shotgun.

I stood back from the hearth and regarded it and the cabin. I was slowly accommodating the possibility that Peterson may indeed have stumbled onto the truth of the Lost Adams Diggings. Next to me, Peterson was scanning the ridges on both sides of the canyon. Pointing at them, he said that there he had spotted sentinels during his earlier visits. I felt a chill run up my spine, for sentinels had been referred to by nearly everyone who entered the canyon in search of the gold. I asked Peterson who he thought the sentinels might be, and he replied that they were Indians. He suspected Apaches but stated that there was evidence that Aztecs, as well as other tribes, had lived in the area in the past.

"They watch over the canyon," he said, "because it is, and has been for a long time, a sacred place to them. It was important to them, and vital to their ceremonies."

I found his observation strange at first, but then I recalled that a number of archeologists are convinced that the Aztecs, who ruled much of central Mexico in generations past, had originally come from the Arizona–New Mexico region. There is also evidence that they returned to this area from time to time to mine gold and silver and harvest precious and semiprecious stones that were then carried back into Mexico to fashion the jewelry and statuary for which they are known. While the Aztecs were renowned for their workmanship and style using gold, it is a fact that the gold they used did not come from the region they dominated in Mexico, and they likely returned to their homeland to mine the ore, perhaps harvesting it from this very canyon.

Deep down, I longed to spot a sentinel or two. After Peterson and I had stared at the ridgelines for several minutes, I said, "I don't see anybody." He replied, "They are there," and walked away.

Thus far, everything had fallen into place. Things still nagged at me, however, and I longed for more evidence, more clues. I told Peterson that, according to the legend, a twelve-foot waterfall should be located upstream some distance away, and beyond that one should be able to discern the old campground of Chief Nana's band of Apaches, the location often referred to as a ceremonial site. Manifesting an impressive calm despite my ongoing doubts and questioning, Peterson said simply, "Follow me." He began walking upstream.

After hiking three hundred yards over rough, rocky terrain, we rounded a sharp bend in the creek, and there, only a few yards in front of me, was a waterfall, a thin stream of clear water cascading down into the pool below and disappearing into the gravel. Another piece of the puzzle had been set in place.

Beckoning me to follow, Peterson led me in a roundabout way from the base of the waterfall to a barely discernable trail that led to a location above. Here we found an expanse of comparatively level ground replete with healthy-looking grass. I saw at once that it would have served as a suitable campsite for a number of Indians: fresh water, signs of game, and enough grass for horses to graze for a time. As I examined the area, it struck me that it was more than a campground; it had the appearance and feeling of a ceremonial spot. A certain undeniable and unexplainable magic surrounded it, and you could easily understand how this location could have been important to the Apaches.

Above the falls, I reminded Peterson, members of Adams's party had found gold nuggets "as big as turkey eggs." I looked longingly at the flowing stream, anxious to inspect its gravels for gold. Peterson told me not to bother, that this part of the stream immediately above the falls, like that below, had been panned out over the years, and the chances of retrieving anything other than trace amounts of gold were minimal.

I had to consider two things, I told Peterson. First, with an enhanced level of diligence, one should still be able to pan gold from this stream, both above and below the falls, retrieving enough to satisfy even the most resistant skeptic that this waterway could have provided the gold harvested by the Adams party. He agreed and claimed he had done just that, finding gold in trace amounts.

The other consideration was this: I stated that the source or sources of the gold, perhaps in the form of an exposed vein or veins that fed the ore into the stream over the past hundreds of thousands, if not millions, of years, was no doubt located farther upstream, somewhere at the higher reaches of this narrowing canyon. I recalled Gotch Ear's comment, as recorded by J. Frank Dobie, that the source of the gold in the stream was an outcrop near the head of Itsnatahey.

While I couldn't ascertain the chances of finding significant gold in the stream at this point, I liked to think that there remained an opportunity to locate the source of the ore. I expressed this notion to Peterson, and he agreed with me. He stated that once he had had a "flash" and seen the gold in "a vein of brown quartz above the falls," but the exact location was vague. He also expressed a strong feeling that there was gold to be found the stream flowing through a smaller canyon that entered this main one from the northwest.

Peterson said he had searched without luck for the vein of gold during an earlier trip to the canyon. I asked him how much time he had spent looking for it, and he confessed that he had only devoted an hour to the task, perhaps less. Not enough, I said, and I was beginning to form plans to return to the area, pack into the canyon, and spend some dedicated time panning up and down the stream for gold. Given time, I would also attempt to locate the source of the ore. The process could take days of exploring. Peterson agreed this was a sensible plan and agreed to accompany me.

We traveled farther up the canyon and reached a high point where we could examine the area. In the near distance I spotted two sugar-cone shaped peaks—the *piloncillos* described by Gotch Ear. When we looked down into the canyon from our perch, we could clearly discern the zigzag pattern of its route.

The day had passed quickly. The sun was already moving westward below the level of the ridges and casting shadows across the canyon. Wanting to be out of the area before dark, we set out down the trail back toward my truck.

As I hiked, I pondered what I had seen, what Peterson had shown me. I had arrived at this canyon a skeptic, prepared to be disappointed. I had expended plenty of time and energy on previous expeditions where I had been led into areas by men who were convinced they had discovered some lost mine or buried treasure. They wanted me to assist in verifying that, indeed, they had made a significant discovery. They also wanted me to write about it, and them. Every one of them had been a waste of time, and I have come to realize that men's hopes and dreams, as well as their egos, often cloud their logic and reasoning. As a professional treasure hunter, I learned to be a skeptic the hard way—by suffering disappointment time and again.

Jim Peterson was different. My journey into this particular canyon with him was also different from previous experiences. It became clear to me that Jim Peterson had no agenda other than to tell the truth. He never talked of the riches he might realize from concentrated panning of this stream. He never once brought up the fame and notoriety he might receive from being written and talked about as the man who had finally located the legendary Lost Adams Diggings.

With Peterson's help, I realized that virtually all the physical and cultural elements—clues if you will—associated with the famous Lost Adams Diggings were here in this canyon. Try as I might to find flaws in his contention that this was indeed the site of the famous lost canyon of gold, I was unable.

As I walked I began making plans to return to the location, with Peterson once again serving as guide. I intended to walk through the entire sequence again, reexamining all the evidence and searching for holes in the hypothesis that this was the location of the Lost Adams Diggings. If all the evidence could be verified and reverified, if all the pieces of the puzzle came together following a subsequent expedition into the area, then I would be prepared, with confidence, to announce the discovery, the solution to the mystery that has perplexed so many for so long, and begin work on a book.

With all that I had to work with, and it was considerable, one remaining piece of the puzzle needed to be accommodated. The truth was, I had nothing until I harvested gold from the stream that wound through this beautiful canyon.

✤ 19 ✤

The Search for the Gold

Before Jim Peterson and I parted ways late on that afternoon of exploring the canyon of gold, we agreed to make plans for a future trip oriented toward panning for the precious metal in the stream. While all the physical and cultural elements associated with Adams's lost canyon pointed to the likelihood that this was indeed the right one, the final proof I still needed entailed finding gold in the stream. If the ore could not be panned from the stream, then a claim of discovering Adams's lost canyon of gold would be incomplete and shallow.

We planned to return to the area with the appropriate equipment and gear to conduct a professional panning operation. If we found gold in the stream, we would then advance farther up the canyon, and perhaps some of its tributaries, in search of the source of the ore. These plans would involve several months of logistical realignment for me to carve out a time between bookings, public appearances, previously arranged treasure-hunting expeditions, and book deadlines. Following a few weeks of communicating back and forth by mail, Peterson and I settled on a date and anticipated another journey to the canyon to pan for gold in selected locations along the streambed as well as to conduct a search for its source.

Regarding the source, the matrix surrounding the gold, probably quartz, eroded over time as a result of weathering and normal breakdown due to alternating freezing and thawing. The gold and the quartz then got pulled inexorably down the slope to be deposited in the stream. Once in Chesser Creek, the material was carried downstream by the flowing water; faster-flowing streams with significant volume transport more material than slower-flowing streams of low volume. More time passed, and the gold was tumbled downstream, down the canyon, and out its mouth, where Chesser Creek joins Chase Creek, which flows from the north, and continues toward the south. Such a process would have taken tens or hundreds of thousands of years, maybe millions. As the gold nuggets saltated downstream, they got worn down from a relatively large size to progressively smaller sizes. The farther from the source, therefore, the smaller the nugget. This smaller nugget was also rounder, with any rough edges worn down by the transportation process. This explained why members of the Adams party found the larger nuggets farther up the canyon above the waterfall.

Chesser Creek experiences extreme variation in flow. There are times when it is completely dry. Following a heavy rain, however, the drainage from the nearby mountains and tributaries fills the stream, increasing its volume as well as its velocity. I have spotted debris such as small limbs and grasses snagged in brush and branches as high as five feet above the creek bed. During times of high water such as this, the relatively heavy gold could be carried downstream with a high degree of efficiency.

According to observations by Peterson and others, the smallest nuggets seen in recent times were panned out of the stream several dozen yards south of the mouth of the canyon. The largest reported were those found by the Adams party above the falls and described as being as large as "a hen's egg."

There was no reason to presume that the exposed vein of gold-laden quartz had been exhausted. If this lode could be found, the ore could likely be extracted with relative ease. That, therefore, became a secondary quest: after ascertaining that gold existed in the stream, the next phase would involve an attempt to locate the source.

As the months passed, Peterson and I communicated often. He had never adapted to e-mail and did not like using the telephone, so he wrote letters, always sending them via certified mail. With time, I noticed a certain urgency in his letters as well as some apparent trembling as he penned them. This was the result of, I suspect, his advancing age and illness. I also learned he had experienced at least one heart attack just prior to our first meeting. Gradually, our plans to return to the canyon of gold began to coalesce. Time was allocated, arrangements were made, and soon the day arrived. Peterson would travel with his wife, a son, and a grandson. The boys would accompany us into the canyon. Mrs. Peterson would remain behind in the truck.

On this trip to the canyon, I invited my wife, Laurie, to come along. As a heretofore unbreakable rule, I never involved family members in my treasure-hunting expeditions for a number of reasons: it is often dangerous; I am generally involved in breaking laws; the fewer people who know what I am doing, the better. In this case, however, the hike into Chesser Gulch offered minimal obstacles and risks. It was a relatively easy trek over gravels, cobbles, and rock-strewn surfaces.

Given the geography of the region, along with observations from Peterson, rattlesnakes offered the only potentially serious threat and were easily dealt with. Peterson shot the snakes when he encountered them. I simply avoided them and removed them from the trail when necessary. The rattlesnakes, after all, were residents of this canyon long before the arrival of human beings in the area, and they are an important element in the ecological web found here.

In addition, I wanted photographs taken of the waterfall, the cabin, the hearth, the stream, the ridges, and other features in the canyon. Laurie is a published writer, a skilled editor, and a professional photographer; her keen eye and talents are always valuable relative to making any book project I decide to indulge in a high-quality endeavor.

We met the Peterson family at a Walmart parking lot in Durango, Colorado, on April 16, 2007. Following a brief breakfast at the snack bar there, we caravanned out of town on Highway 160 to Cortez, where we turned onto Highway 666, the Devil's Highway, southward into New Mexico. (Highway 666 has since been renamed Highway 491 as a result of an outcry from fundamentalist Christians bothered by perceived biblical implications.)

We followed Highway 666 into Gallup, where we left it and turned west on Interstate 40 into Arizona. Only a few miles over the border, we turned south onto Highway 191. With stops for lunch, gas, mechanical problems with the Peterson vehicle, and Peterson's need to use the bathroom often, we finally arrived in Springerville, Arizona, in time to check into a motel. Peterson was seventy-nine years old at the time and suffering from prostate cancer.

Following a restful night, Laurie and I met the Peterson family for breakfast the next morning in the café attached to the motel. It became immediately clear that Peterson was not well. He'd had difficulty sleeping during the night, manifested weakness, and was urinating blood. He was shaking and had fallen into a state of depression. Following a family discussion, the Petersons decided to take him home and get him to a hospital. Laurie and I agreed to continue on to the canyon. After bidding the Peterson family good-bye, we drove away—they traveled back north, and Laurie and I headed south.

Following Highway 191 southward out of Springerville, we passed through the picturesque small towns of Nutrioso, Alpine, and Hannigan Meadows. The road wound through the scenic and arresting mountains comprising a portion of the Apache-Sitgreaves National Forest.

Later that morning, as we began to descend out of the higher reaches of the mountain range and toward the mining company town of Morenci, I advised Laurie that we were on the lookout for the entrance to Adams's fabled lost canyon of gold, which would be on the left. We passed a few minor landmarks familiar to me from the last visit to the region, but before I could spot the mouth of the canyon and make the turnoff, I found myself in the zone of the bustling copper-mining activity of the former Phelps Dodge Corporation in Morenci, now owned by Freeport-McMoRan. Embarrassed, I told Laurie I had missed the turnoff. I turned around, and we retraced the route back up the canyon. When I was convinced I had gone too far, I admitted again to having missed the entrance. Twice more we drove along the road in search of the barely noticeable turnoff, where we would park at the entrance. By now, something was nagging at me; something was not quite right, but I could not explain what it was. Then I discovered the problem.

Along a several-hundred-yard stretch of Highway 191, a chain-link fence topped by angled barbed wire ran along the east side of the road. Attached to the chain link every forty yards were metal signs proclaiming, "No Trespassing: Violators Will Be Prosecuted." Driving slowly, I regarded the fence and wondered why it had been built. Fences are constructed to either keep something in or keep something out. The presence of barbed wire angled outward, along with the warning signs, suggested this fence was intended to keep people out. I suddenly realized that the road we were driving over was new—it was not the same Highway 191 I had driven several months earlier when Peterson and I visited the canyon. Then it occurred to me: the road had been moved.

I pulled to the western side of the highway opposite the fence, parked, and got out. Laurie opted to remain in the truck. Crossing the road I reached the chin-link barricade and looked beyond it down the slope toward the drainage pattern. In the creek and out of sight of drivers on this new portion of the highway, there was a bustle of activity: men moving about, one carrying a sheaf of what appeared to be blueprints; heavy equipment moving up and down the creek, changing and rearranging its contours; flatbed trucks hauling equipment in through a gated entrance located toward the south; a trailer serving as an office and identified as belonging to the Freeport-McMoRan mining company.

As I stood by the fence, fingers curled into the chain link, I examined the terrain on the other side of the creek and spotted what I was looking for—the entrance to Adams's canyon. Suddenly, I understood what was going on: Freeport-McMoRan, the successor to the Phelps Dodge mining corporation, which it had recently purchased, had discovered the gold in Chase Creek and was in the process of restricting access to it. The entrance to the canyon had been sealed off, and Chesser Creek was made inaccessible to anyone other than mining company employees.

The Phelps Dodge Corporation, located at this site for decades, had long been associated with the mining of copper and a number of other important minerals. Not many people are aware, however, that it had also long been active in mining and processing gold. Gold has been found throughout most of the mountain ranges in the area. It had been only a matter of time before some geologist with the mining company discovered the gold in Chesser Creek. I later encountered company documents associated with Freeport-McMoRan that identified the company as now specializing in mining copper and gold as its principal activities.

If I had harbored any doubts whatsoever relative to what was happening below, they were erased with the arrival of an unexpected vehicle. A light-colored pickup truck approached and slowed, finally stopping next to where I was standing by the fence. Two men inside wore what appeared to be uniforms. I immediately spotted two shotguns hanging from a rear-window gun rack. On the side of the truck was a logo for a private security firm. After rolling down the passenger-side window, the two men glared at me, managing their most menacing looks as they instructed me to leave the area immediately. I wanted to ask them questions about what was going on down at the creek but instead only nodded and retreated to my own vehicle.

I explained to Laurie what I had seen and the reason for the barbed-wire-topped fence and the patrol. There was only one reason for such tight security. It had nothing to do with the mining of copper. Freeport-McMoRan was mining gold. As we discussed the situation, another security truck drove by. I checked my watch and made a note that the patrols passed by every fifteen minutes.

This new situation heightened the challenge of obtaining entrance to the canyon to search for the presumed exposed vein of gold. Days later I wrote to Peterson about the situation I had encountered. He expressed some disappointment but not defeat. We would, he said, find another way to get into the area. As Laurie and I drove away, I began formulating plans to return to the location another time. In addition, I began to consider ways to overcome the obstacles of the fence and the armed guards when next I arrived.

✤ 20 ✤

Entry

More time passed, and before I was prepared, the year 2008 had already arrived. My intention was to plan for a spring return to Chesser Gulch while it was still cool in the mountains and the threat of rattlesnakes was at a minimum.

Since the previous visit, Peterson and I had exchanged more letters. He informed me of the state of his health. It was not good; the bout of sickness he experienced during the earlier trip had left him weak and unable to travel. He continued to sound depressed and was having episodes of falling as well as severe headaches. On two occasions, dates were set to travel to the canyon, but each time he had to beg off for health reasons. More time went by without the logistics coming together properly.

While I was awaiting some definitive response from Peterson, my research revealed that Freeport-McMoRan had acquired Phelps Dodge Morenci, Inc., on March 19, 2007. Prior to the purchase, Phelps Dodge was regarded as one of the largest copper-mining corporations in the world. According to Freeport-McMoRan's informational release, the company mines a wide selection of ores in this mineral-rich part of Arizona, including iron, tungsten, molybdenum, cobalt, tantalum, platinum, vermiculite, thorium, kyanite, antimony, zirconium, titanium, uranium, silver, lead, zinc, tin, and manganese. The greatest percentage of its mining activity, as well as its profit, according to company documents, is associated with copper and gold.

More time passed, and arranging a trip to the canyon encountered numerous logistical difficulties. Then, Jim Peterson passed away on March 31, 2009. He was eighty-two years old. I would return to the canyon alone.

In late April I arrived at the section of Highway 191, also known as the Coronado Trail, where Chesser Gulch was blocked off by the chain-link fence. A few dozen yards north of the limits of the fence was a pullout on the west side of the road, a place where the security vehicles turned around before making a return pass across the area. I parked there, between the highway and where Chase Creek passed on the west side of the road, and studied my options relative to gaining access to the canyon. I immediately deduced at least two ways to breach security but decided against doing so. I determined to seek another route, a legal one, into the canyon.

I studied the maps of the area I had accumulated. They indicated that the mid- to upper levels of the canyon were on land that belonged to the US Forest Service. With the assistance of Google Earth, I located a bladed road—called the Grand Enchantment Trail, according to the Forest Service map—that wound through Forest Service land and traversed a low ridge that overlooked the canyon from the northwest. Along this road—which was neither grand nor enchanted but in dreadful condition—was a trailhead, with the trail leading from the ridge down a drainage area and into Chesser Gulch. This access demanded investigation; if it proved a safe and legal way to enter Chesser Gulch, then it would facilitate movement into and out of the canyon, and no clear trespassing ordinances would be violated.

I negotiated the bladed road, which clearly was not used much, and found a turnout where I could park my truck. From that point I walked to the trailhead and immediately located the trail that wound down into the canyon. Like the bladed road, the trail had not been used much in recent years and in places seemed to disappear altogether. Finally, after a hike of just over an hour, I arrived at the Apache ceremonial ground above the falls.

My intention on arriving was to pan the stream for gold to ascertain that indeed this precious metal could be found there. Since I was already at the confluence of three canyons, whose runoff fed Chesser Creek, I decided to forego panning for the time being to investigate their upper reaches. I intended to identify potential panning sites but also wanted to get a close-up look at the rock outcrops at the higher levels. It was in one or more of these that the Adams gold had originated.

It was a pleasant day. I enjoyed the sounds of the canyon—the singing of birds, the chatter of squirrels, the hum of insects—as I worked my way upstream. Now and again I heard a hoof fall on rock as deer made their way farther up the canyon ahead of me. As I walked by the narrow stream, I imagined Adams and his party of miners squatting along its edge as they panned for the gold they were so excited to find.

I had proceeded perhaps one hundred yards up the stream beyond the waterfall when I was seized by a peculiar sensation: I had the feeling that I was being watched. During previous treasure-hunting expeditions in Mexico I had experienced the same kind of impression—that my movements were being observed by someone unknown. In every case, it turned out that I was correct. I was experiencing the same feeling at that moment.

I looked back down the stream and beyond the waterfall to see if someone had entered the canyon behind me and was following. I perceived no movement or sound. I examined the route I had taken into the canyon from the ridge and found nothing there either. There was no one. I listened closely for the sound of footfalls on the gravelly and rocky substrate. Nothing. Then I thought of Peterson's mention of sentinels watching him from the ridges during his visits to the canyon. My eyes darted to the tops of the canyon walls surrounding me. I searched them from left to right and back again. I repeated the motion. Here and there I saw shadows that struck me as suspicious, particularly one near the top of the southeastern rim. If someone were watching me, I did not want him to know that I was looking for him or had spotted him, so I did not let my gaze linger. A moment later, when I looked back at the same spot, the shadow was gone.

Putting the notion that someone might be watching me out of my mind, I continued my search for evidence of the vein of gold. Though I searched diligently for the next hour, I found nothing encouraging. As I made my way up the canyon, I could not shake the feeling that someone, or maybe more than one person, was observing my movements.

I reached the upper limits of the ever-narrowing canyon and turned to make my way back down, continuing with my search. Now and again some promising location would send me scurrying up a slope to investigate, but each time I returned with negative results. By the time I made it back to the waterfall, the feeling of being watched had become stronger than ever. Raising my canteen to my lips, I lifted my eyes once again to the ridge tops to see if I could spot an observer. Once again, nothing. Most of the day had passed before I realized I had little time left for any concentrated panning activity. It would have to wait until I could make another trip to the canyon.

During the next hour and a half I made my way out of the canyon, slowly, deliberately, finally arriving at the location where I had parked my truck. I was never able to shake the feeling that I was being observed, but I never saw or heard anyone. Was it merely the power of suggestion, the result of Peterson's tale of being watched by sentinels he perceived to be Indians? Or was it real? The truth was, I did not know.

As I drove out of the area, on the first leg of my journey home I replayed the events of the day in my mind. I was disappointed not to find the vein of gold, but I had been thwarted in similar searches in the past. Such a thing was not unusual—if easy to locate, the vein of gold would have been discovered long ago. It would simply require a more intensive search of the canyons, perhaps several.

I inventoried all the evidence I had gathered in favor of Chesser Gulch being the canyon associated with the Lost Adams Diggings. I reviewed what I could recall of accounts of earlier searches for the canyon by others, their observations, and the things Peterson had told me.

A successful investigator never takes any of the available evidence for granted and constantly reviews every item, as well as any possible alternatives, time and again, before coming to any kind of conclusion. My experience has been that if one does this enough times, a pattern will emerge. Patterns can lead to conclusions. During the next two days of travel back to my home, I finally arrived at a conclusion and my reasons for it. But before making a final analysis, I determined that another trip to the canyon was necessary. This time, I would refrain from searching for the source of the gold and concentrate on panning. I was certain that gold could be found in the stream, but I had to see it for myself. I had to feel the flakes and nuggets between my fingers. It was the last missing element involved in the complete solution of the mystery of the location of the fabled Lost Adams Diggings.

✢ 21 ✢

Gold!

Before I got home from the trip to Adams's lost canyon, I was already making plans for another visit. I arrived at several objectives over the next few days.

First, I wanted to return and engage in some fact-checking. I had decided that I was going to write a book about the Lost Adams Diggings, my research and investigation into locating it, and the ultimate discovery—or more properly, rediscovery. I needed to retrace my steps and make certain that I remembered everything correctly: distances, directions, landmarks, and more.

Second, intrigued by the notion of that special piece of landscape serving as a ceremonial ground for the Apaches and other Indians, I wanted to get a closer look at it; I wanted to spend some time there and become better acquainted with the site.

Third, for my investigation to be complete, I needed to find gold in the stream, the same stream from which Adams and the miners had harvested a fortune in nuggets. I had earlier identified a number of potential sites along the stream from which I intended to pan for the precious metal. Given time after panning, I would again attempt to explore the upper reaches of the main canyon and its tributaries to try to locate one or more sources of the gold that found its way into the stream.

The more I engaged in planning the return expedition to the canyon, the more I realized I needed another pair of eyes. I wanted to bring someone along who was familiar with the legend of the diggings and could scrutinize my observations, analyze my conclusions, and provide unbiased, learned, and professional opinions. I wanted someone along who would not be afraid to challenge my conclusions if necessary.

Other than my regular partners, with whom I had worked for over three decades and engaged in around two hundred expeditions in search of lost mines and buried treasures, I had rarely had anyone accompany me. Since two of my longtime partners were dead and the third had retired from the search, I invited a new colleague, Earl Theiss, to go along with me. Theiss had a great deal of experience panning for gold, far more than I, and could claim uncountable successes. Since this was a placer deposit I thought he would be an ideal choice. Furthermore, Theiss was a competent rock man with a good pair of eyes. He could spot things that escape the notice of most people. A good set of eyes in the kind of geological environment we would be entering was crucial. Last, Theiss was already intimate with the story of the Lost Adams Diggings in all its versions and with all of the various locations identified as the actual canyon. He could offer objective and honest criticism of my observations, which I eagerly anticipated.

More time passed as schedules and bookings, as well as other elements of life, interfered with finalizing plans to return to the canyon. Prior to setting out for Arizona, Theiss and I spent some time examining Google Earth imagery as well as up-to-date topographic maps of the area to achieve a greater intimacy. Since we would be hiking to predetermined locations, we packed light, carrying the necessary water and food, snake sticks, and panning equipment with the related digging tools. We departed our homes at 7:00 a.m. on November 15, 2013. Around mid-morning of the second day, we arrived at the Forest Service trail that provided access to the canyon of gold.

As before, the trail we hiked from the ridge into the canyon was rough, rocky, and covered with brush and bramble; it appeared not to have been used for at least two decades, save for the last time I traveled it. Though it was November and the weather was cool, we kept an eye out for rattlesnakes. They tend to den up this time of year but often come out during the warmth of the day. Despite the somewhat difficult trek, we arrived at a position a short distance upstream from the waterfall in a little over an hour. Another few minutes of hiking took us straight to the falls and the Indian ceremonial ground located above them.

Theiss examined the area and concurred that it could have served as a sacred site. The Stonehenge-like natural rock formation functioned as a perfect backdrop. The entire site, in fact, had a certain aura of unexplainable enchantment about it. Satisfied with our interpretation and anxious to examine the rest of the immediate area of the canyon, we were unprepared for what followed. Rounding the southeastern end of the rock formation, Theiss spotted something I had overlooked on previous trips. There, on a flat, smooth, vertical outcrop of rock was an amazing pictograph: a primitive rendering of a shaman. The figure was not unlike the depictions of shamans in the Pecos River valley of West Texas, as well as in other locations throughout the American West. The shaman, a priestlike individual found among some of the world's oldest cultures, is associated with magic, healing, and other skills. Shamanism was a type of spirituality practiced among the North American Indian tribes.

The presence of the shaman pictograph fortified the hypothesis that the site was sacred, not only to the Warm Springs Apache band of Chief Nana but for visitors to the canyon perhaps as many as five thousand years earlier, according to archeologists. Theiss's keen eyes were already paying off.

We then examined the area around the waterfall for several minutes and took a few photographs. Runoff from recent rains had filled the stream, and the flow was significant. Consequently the water coming off the falls was correspondingly impressive. During at least one previous trip, as a result of a prolonged drought, the stream had been relatively dry, and the waterfall amounted to only a trickle. Proceeding downstream, we eventually came upon the extant cabin built atop the one set aflame by the Apaches a century and a half earlier. I showed Theiss the hearth and pointed out the secret chambers. Since my last visit to the canyon, someone had torn much of the structure apart, but the chambers were still discernible. The rocks that had once made up part of the fireplace and chimney were scattered several feet in all directions. I did spot the slab that once covered the secret chamber beneath the hearth.

While Theiss looked around, examined the creek, and explored a bit farther downstream, I busied myself with more fact-checking and took a few notes. Later, I joined him, and we continued to explore downstream for a short distance, stopping now and then to scoop some gravel out of the creek for examination. While we found promising signs, we found no gold. This, after all, was part of the creek that had been extensively panned over the generations.

Satisfied that we had accomplished all that we could in this section of the canyon, we moved upstream, panning here and there along the way but still finding nothing. Above the waterfall, we entered an unnamed tributary canyon that zigzagged in a generally eastern direction. Another seldom-used trail wound up into the canyon, paralleling the narrow stream that drained runoff. After several minutes of climbing, we agreed to take a break and sought shade in an inviting cluster of thick oak trees. As we munched on trail food and drank from our canteens, we examined this portion of the stream. Theiss pointed to a promising spot and began pulling a gold pan and digging tools from his pack. After removing several large rocks and excavating through a few inches of the stream gravel, he withdrew several handfuls of the material and placed them in the pan. Several minutes of swirling the gravels around and eliminating the worthless pebbles yielded nothing. Theiss dug an inch or two deeper and extracted more of the gravels. More swirling, more elimination of nonessential material, but no gold.

Despite not finding gold, I had a good feeling about this location. I encouraged Theiss to go deeper. A third pan full. Nothing. On the fourth try, however, Theiss let out a whoop and pointed to a flake of gold in the pan. On the fifth try, more flakes appeared, each one larger than the first. Gold! We had finally found it.

Satisfied that this canyon was at least one of the tributaries that provided gold to Chesser Creek, we returned to the junction and traveled one hundred yards up the principal drainage for the stream, far upstream from where we were convinced the waterway had been panned out. Here, we stopped to pan a previously identified location that appeared to hold promise. This time we found gold after the third try and in sufficient quantity and size to provide a level of comfort that we had resolved the final piece of the mystery. Given all the evidence, given all the inductive and deductive reasoning and logic necessary to arrive at an honest and reliable conclusion, and given the application of time and energy to panning the stream, we had finally connected all the dots with the discovery of gold. There was no longer any doubt: we were standing in Adams's lost canyon of gold, and in the shallow, narrow stream at our feet lay a fortune in gold nuggets.

✤ 22 ✤

The Elusive Source

With the harvesting of gold from the shallow stream that was the setting of the Lost Adams Diggings, only one more mystery remained to be solved: the location of the source, or sources, of the ore. Somewhere up two or more of the canyons that fed Chesser Creek were outcrops likely composed of gold-laced quartz.

Finding the source of the gold in the stream had never been crucial to determining the precise location of the Lost Adams Diggings. It would simply be an additional quest to layer atop an already satisfying and productive adventure.

These outcrops might be found anywhere in the upper reaches of the canyons. Though we searched for hours, we found nothing. It was possible that the source of the gold was an outcrop not in one of the canyon walls but in an upper creek bottom itself. As a result of the deposition of gravels transported by the recent rains and heavy runoff, the possibility existed that it was covered over. Another rainfall followed by the surging stream could very well remove the cover of rock debris, exposing the vein beneath. Such are the vagaries of nature.

Accepting that we had accomplished all that we could for the time being, we hoisted our packs and made our way back up the rugged trail to where we had parked the truck, all the while making plans to return.

On the way out of the canyon, I thought about Jim Peterson and experienced a pang of sadness that he was not with us to share in the adventure. I also wished he could have been involved in the plans to reenter the canyon and pan for the gold we now knew was still there.

At this writing, more plans are being formulated to return to the canyon to pan more of the gold from a number of promising locations in the stream. In addition, we intend to conduct yet another search for the source of the gold that furnishes the ore to this small waterway. Realistically, however, we must accept that the chances of finding it are minimal. The truth is, it may never be found.

It is a documented fact that many others have panned gold from the little stream since the time Adams and the miners visited the area. Surely it occurred to those placer miners that the sources of the gold lay somewhere in the rocks in the upper reaches of one or more of the canyons. Given that, they certainly went looking for them. There is no evidence that they were never found.

It is also a certainty that since Phelps Dodge and Freeport-McMoRan geologists knew of the gold in the lower reaches of Chesser Creek at its confluence with Chase Creek, they would have undertaken a search for the sources. If they had found anything they would have, without delay, established a sophisticated mining operation at the site to harvest this gold. There is no evidence of such at this time.

Thus, the fact remains that the sources of the gold that made famous the Lost Adams Diggings have yet to be discovered. Such a notion offers hope for an opportunity for a future quest. In the meantime, the upper reaches of Chesser Creek are still yielding impressive harvests of gold, a legacy of the Lost Adams Diggings.

✤ 23 ✤

Review, Analysis, and Conclusions

The quest for well over a century was to determine the exact location of the Lost Adams Diggings, a mystery that has baffled
hundreds, if not thousands, over the decades. It has lured many to
search for the legendary lost placer mine; it has been the quest of
treasure hunters, adventurers, truth seekers, historians, and other
interested parties.

Prior to Jim Peterson's odd rediscovery of the Lost Adams
Diggings in Chesser Gulch in southeastern Arizona's Graham
County, the only other general location that was ever given serious consideration was the Datil Mountains in west-central New
Mexico. Most searchers devoted their attention to this latter location for a variety of reasons, all spurious. Despite the hundreds
who searched for Adams's canyon of gold in that particular geographic location, not a single shred of evidence indicating it might
be the correct location, compelling or otherwise, was ever found.
Nonetheless, the area was never rejected, and searchers insisted on
concentrating on this mountain range.

A situation such as this, wherein two hypothesized locations
are presented for consideration, requires undertaking something
rarely done in studies of lost mines and buried treasure: historical
investigation. Historical investigation applies appropriate research
methodologies in the resolution of a historical conundrum.

With the Lost Adams Diggings, we have long had a mystery and a challenge: Was the true site of the rich lost canyon of gold, as many people believed, in the Datil Mountains of west-central New Mexico? Many who claimed to have immersed themselves in research pertaining to the lost canyon of gold long embraced the proposition that it was. Their research, we have come to learn, invariably amounted to reading what others had written and accepting it at face value. The truth is, precious little true research has been undertaken on the Lost Adams Diggings, resulting in perpetuation of the mistaken observations and conclusions of others. Until now there has been no historical investigation whatsoever.

The true location of the Lost Adams Diggings was found in an entirely different place, in southeastern Arizona. This site was recently identified through rigorous examination of distance, direction, and geographic considerations, not to mention a long-needed dose of logic, common sense, and empirical observation.

Procedurally, the investigation of a historical mystery may involve one or more applicable hypotheses. In the case of the Lost Adams Diggings, the prevailing hypothesis for well over a century has been that the lost canyon of gold could be found in the Datil Mountains. Surprisingly, this hypothesis has never been tested, analyzed, questioned, or even given much thought. The record shows that it has, for the most part, been blindly accepted by any and all who have pursued the quest of locating the famous lost mine.

In addition to conducting an appropriate investigation into the mystery, the true researcher is also faced with separating the truth from the myth. In a number of aspects related to the Lost Adams Diggings story, fact and myth blend, but there remain obvious examples of myth being substituted for truth. The task of the investigator is to determine what to discard as myth and retain as truth.

As a result of the only organized and logical research and investigation ever applied to the conundrum, a revised working hypothesis has evolved: "The Lost Adams Diggings will be found somewhere in the southeastern quadrant of the state of Arizona. A corollary to this hypothesis is that the Lost Adams Diggings will *not* be found in the Datil Mountains."

Normally, the evidence-gathering phase of an investigation is preceded by analysis that ultimately dictates what evidence one pursues. Hypothesis is the most important mental technique of the investigator, and its main function is to suggest new experiments or new observations. Explorations and observations are then carried out with the deliberate objective of testing the hypothesis. Hypotheses should be used as tools to uncover facts, to identify truths. They are not ends in themselves.

The goal of the investigator is the development of proof in favor of the hypothesis, proof that is sufficient to solve the problem. A preponderance of the evidence would be represented in historical matters by the establishment of the preferred hypothesis. Basically, this would mean arriving at one hypothesis, among all of those that can be advanced, which appears to account for all the evidence, or at least explains more data than the competing hypothesis (or hypotheses). When more than one hypothesis is proposed to account for the known facts, the preferred hypothesis can be determined by invoking Occam's razor. Named for William of Ockham, the influential fourteenth-century philosopher, Occam's razor affirms that the simplest and clearest explanation—that is, the hypothesis with the fewest assumptions—is most likely to be correct and is to be preferred. None of this has ever been undertaken relative to the Lost Adams Diggings.

Therefore, given the complete absence of evidence in support of the long-predominant hypothesis related to the supposed Datil Mountains location, the formulation of a second one is necessary to solve the problem and answer the question relative to the location of the Lost Adams Diggings. The hypothesis is as follows: "Chesser Gulch, and its associated tributaries, located in the Davis Mountains in Graham County of southeastern Arizona, is the site of the legendary Lost Adams Diggings."

This hypothesized location is a long way geographically from the traditionally accepted one, but thus far it is the only one that survives logical and sophisticated investigation. The initial assumptions provided by the Chesser Gulch location have been replaced by evidence gathered on site, all of it lending support for the acceptance of the hypothesis. The evidence includes the following:

1. The remains were found of a log cabin that had been constructed many years prior to the one more recently erected at the site. The comparatively wide floor of the canyon there is the only suitable place along its entire length for a dwelling and a corral. The remains of an earlier cabin, found at a depth in the soil of less than one foot, reveal that it had been burned. One small, charred piece of log that had been unearthed had an arrow point embedded in it. Thus, we have clear evidence of an earlier cabin along with the compelling suggestion of an Indian attack.

2. There was a rock hearth of considerable age at the location of the cabin, one that possessed not one but two secret chambers—one at the rear of the hearth and another, larger one beneath it.

3. According to all the versions of the Lost Adams Diggings, a waterfall twelve feet high was to be found a short distance upstream from the cabin site. Approximately three hundred yards up the canyon from the site of the aforementioned cabin is a waterfall, twelve feet high.

4. Beyond the waterfall, according to all the versions of the tale, was the location where Chief Nana and his band of Apaches camped, apparently for extended periods. It has been referred to as a "sacred" place by the Apaches. In fact, above the aforementioned waterfall lies a relatively extensive open space quite suitable for

a campground. At this location can be found a healthy growth of grasses upon which the horses of the Indians could have grazed for a time. Here, a number of artifacts have been found suggesting that it was indeed used as an Indian campground in the past.

5. The presence of a centuries-old pictograph of a shaman in this same location indicates that it was more than a campground; the site strongly suggests that it was used as a ceremonial ground.

6. From a higher elevation upstream from the waterfall, one can look down onto Chesser Gulch, where the cabin is located, and discern an obvious zigzag pattern to the shape of the canyon, corresponding with one of the most commonly cited characterizations of the location.

7. From this same elevated location, one can also discern two prominent peaks not far away. These landforms match the description of the *piloncillos*, the two sugar-cone-shaped mountains described to Adams by Gotch Ear.

8. Some Lost Adams Diggings enthusiasts have made a point of dwelling on a clue referred to as the "point of the Malpais," which makes no sense when considering the Datil Mountains location. On the other hand, located less than a half mile east of Chesser Gulch, one finds a landform named Malpais Mountain. This is indicated on US Geological Survey maps as well as on Google Earth. From a location in the gulch, the peak, or point, of Malpais Mountain can be seen.

9. The most important piece of evidence relating to this being the location of the Lost Adams Diggings is the fact that there is gold in the stream that runs through the canyon. Evidence exists that this stream was panned often and successfully for well over a century.

Even today, evidence of gold harvesting can be found along the creek in the form of residue from dry wash operations. Finally, proof that gold exists in the creek in significant quantity was acquired during a panning operation in November 2013.

It is necessary to point out here that the landscapes in the area of this canyon have changed dramatically since Adams's time. Some landforms and locational indicators quoted by others do not exist today as a result of road construction, ranching activities, and the extensive open-pit and other types of mining nearby, which have relocated billions of tons of earth.

And there is this: In a book little known and often overlooked by searchers for and researchers of the Lost Adams Diggings, *Ghost Towns of the West*, author Lambert Florin provides details relative to the settling of Alma, New Mexico. Among his historical gems, he mentions that early Alma settler W. H. McCullough, along with Captain J. G. Birney and another man, decided one day in the late 1870s to ride over "to the Lost Adams Diggings in Arizona to see what was going on there." An important geographical point to make here is that Chesser Gulch is only twenty-five straight-line miles southwest of Alma. This locational reference predates the observations presented by J. Frank Dobie and others and dovetails with the Chesser Gulch hypothesis.

For more than 150 years, the prevalent hypothesis among a number of writers, as well as professional and amateur treasure hunters, has been "The Lost Adams Diggings is located somewhere in the Datil Mountains." The question this begs is, What evidence has been offered to support this hypothesis? The answer is none.

Sometimes just as important as providing evidence of where something is located is providing evidence of where it is not located. As a result of extensive readings and research accompanied by empirical observation, I contend that the oft-repeated and long-accepted notion of the Datil Mountains as the location of the Lost Adams Diggings is in error. Related to that contention, I suggest there exists no competent evidence whatsoever to support such a hypothesis. Furthermore, anyone who simply took the time to examine it relative to the conditions of distance, direction, time, and geography would easily conclude that the choice of this location is absurd on a number of levels and that the hypothesis must be rejected. Key points utilized in rejecting the Datil Mountains as the location of the Lost Adams Diggings include the following:

1. The distance between the Datil Mountains (the destination) and Gila Bend, Arizona (the origin) is simply too great to have been traveled during the time frame provided by Adams and others. I will go one step further: given all the evidence available, along with a healthy dose of logic and common sense, it would have been impossible for the Adams party to have traveled that distance from Gila Bend to the Datil Mountains in west-central New Mexico over rugged and difficult terrain during the stated time span.

2. The Adams party panned gold in a canyon inhabited by a band of Warm Springs Apaches. The area of southeastern Arizona, including Chesser Gulch, was homeland to this particular tribe. The effective northern limit of the range of the Warm Springs Apaches was the headwaters of the San Francisco River. The Datil Mountains were rarely, if ever, visited by Apaches, Warm Springs or otherwise. These mountains were part of the homeland of the Zuni Indians. Thus, it is beyond reason to suggest that any party of miners, or anyone else, would have encountered Warm Springs Apaches in the Datil Mountains.

3. There has never been found in the Datil Mountains a site, a canyon, or a stream that satisfied the criteria for the location of the Lost Adams Diggings. In fact, no one has ever found a canyon anywhere that satisfied the distance, directional, and geographic criteria to the degree that Chesser Gulch does. There exists the likelihood that there are other canyons in Arizona and New Mexico that have yielded placer gold, but they are not the Lost Adams Diggings.

4. When Adams conducted subsequent searches for the lost canyon of gold, he never once traveled to the Datil Mountains. Most of his personal searches were focused on locations in the general geographic area of Clifton, Arizona.

5. The choice of the Datil Mountains as the location of the Lost Adams Diggings is based on the observations and descriptions of only two men, neither of whom possessed any credibility whatsoever relative to this quest.

Therefore, given the analysis of distance, direction, time, and geography pertinent to the Lost Adams Diggings, hypothesis number two, that the rich placer mine is located somewhere in the Datil Mountains, must be rejected. This is the only logical determination. Further, the Datil Mountains provide no evidence of being the location of the lost canyon of gold whatsoever, only assumptions, none of which are clear, and none of which can be supported.

I anticipate that this conclusion will be met with opposition, antagonism, and rejection from the traditionalists who support the notion that the Datil Mountains hold the key to the location of the Lost Adams Diggings. Indeed, I have already experienced such responses. However, when I challenge those who cling to the traditional viewpoint to debate, to compare evidence, and to discuss all the available hypotheses, they retreat into the seclusion of pre-determined notions and refuse my invitation. I cannot remember the wag who first voiced this observation, but I am grateful for it: the truth will set you free, but before it does it generally upsets and aggravates you. At this stage of the discussion of the Lost Adams Diggings, the traditionalists appear to be upset and aggravated. Disappointingly, they are also silent.

Anyone who professes an interest in history will also possess a passion for learning, sharing, and disseminating the truth. After all, isn't truth the objective of historical research? To deny such a pursuit, to remain blind to the evidence and to refuse to examine and discuss it, is not part of the makeup of one who is legitimately and morally interested in the truth.

In the end, assuming and invoking the spirit of determining the truth, I will continue to attempt to make contributions to the body of knowledge associated with the Lost Adams Diggings. Readers, one and all, are invited to accompany me on this special journey.

In addition, I will continue to journey to Chesser Creek, the true location of the legendary Lost Adams Diggings, and harvest the plentiful gold that can still be found in the stream.

Selected Bibliography

Allen, Charles. *The Adams Diggings Story.* El Paso, TX: Hughes-Buie Company, 1935.

Byerts, W. H. *Gold: The Adams Gold Diggings.* Self-published, 1919.

Campbell, Joseph. *The Hero with a Thousand Faces.* Princeton, NJ: Princeton University Press, 1973.

Campbell, Joseph (with Bill Moyers). *The Power of Myth.* New York: Doubleday, 1988.

Dobie, J. Frank. *Apache Gold and Yaqui Silver.* New York: Bramhall House, 1938.

Florin, Lambert. *Ghost Towns of the West.* New York: Promontory Press, 1970.

French, Richard. *Four Days from Fort Wingate: The Lost Adams Diggings.* Caldwell, ID: Caxton Press, Ltd., 1994.

Jameson, W. C. *Buried Treasures of the American Southwest.* Little Rock, AR: August House Publishers, 1989.

———. *Lost Mines and Buried Treasures of Arizona.* Albuquerque: University of New Mexico Press, 2009.

———. *New Mexico Treasure Tales.* Caldwell, ID: Caxton Press. 2003.

McKenna, James A. *Black Range Tales.* New York: Wilson-Erickson, Inc., 1936.

Mitchell, John D. *Lost Mines of the Great Southwest.* Phoenix, AZ: Journal Company, Inc., 1935.

Purcell, Jack. *The Lost Adams Diggings: Myth, Mystery, and Madness.* Placitas, NM: Nine Lives Press, 2003.

Smith, C. C. "More about the Lost Adams Gold Diggings," *Frontier Times* 5, no. 6 (March 1928): 318–19.

Tenny, A. M. "The Lost Adams Gold Diggings," *Frontier Times* 5, no. 6 (March 1928): 240–48.

Vogler, Christopher. *The Writer's Journey.* 2nd ed. Studio City, CA: Michael Wise Productions, 1998.

A few other books devoted to the Lost Adams Diggings have been published over the years, but none contribute to the understanding of the legend and lore, the geography, the chronology, and the related history any better than those mentioned above. In addition to these listed standard sources of information on the Lost Adams Diggings, the Internet is replete with observations and writings. They range from sophisticated and detailed to dreadful, and it is up to the researcher to separate the wheat from the chaff.

Acknowledgments

Heartfelt thanks to the late Jim Peterson, who first guided me into Adams's lost canyon of gold. Peterson was a nice man and a pleasant companion, a man who was dedicated to perpetuating the truth, and I wish he could have lived long enough to celebrate the finalization of the quest.

Earl Theiss is one of the most competent prospectors I have ever met. His trips with me to the lost canyon always yielded priceless information and findings. His attention to detail and his powers of analysis and deduction are impressive. His competencies as a researcher and a treasure hunter are admirable, and I anticipate future quests in his company.

Laurie Jameson is a skilled and experienced editor who performs her special magic on any and every manuscript she works on. She has edited everything from collections of poetry to *New York Times* best-selling fiction. I am lucky and grateful that she finds time to edit my work.

Index

About the Author

W. C. Jameson is the award-winning author of more than 100 books. A professional treasure hunter for over five decades, he has led or participated in over two hundred expeditions in the United States and Mexico. Jameson has served as a consultant to the television and film industry and has appeared on the Discovery Channel, the History Channel, the Travel Channel, National Public Radio, and *Nightline*.

Lightning Source UK Ltd.
Milton Keynes UK
UKHW021323170921
390742UK00008B/1460